# Contemporary British Cinema

## a teacher's guide

### Mike Kirkup

Auteur

## Mike Kirkup

spent 14 years in the culture/exhibition sector working at the Tyneside Cinema in Newcastle as Education Officer and Film Programmer. He is currently working on a number of film education projects across the North East.

## With thanks to...

John Atkinson at *Auteur* for his patience, advice and for re-defining the word 'deadline'.

Jonny Tull, keeper of the priceless Tyneside Cinema archives and everyone at that wonderful institution.

All my friends and colleagues past and present working in the cultural exhibition sector across the UK.

And, with love, my wife Sarah, without whom I would not have had the chance to do this work. Corny, I know, but you complete me.

First Published 2004

by Auteur

The Old Surgery, 9 Pulford Road, Leighton Buzzard, Bedfordshire LU7 1AB

© Auteur Publishing, 2004

ISBN 1 903663 28 8

Auteur on the internet: http://www.auteur.co.uk

Designed and typeset by Loaf, PO Box 737, Cottenham, Cambridge CB4 8BA

Printed by The Direct Printing Company, Brixworth, Northamptonshire

# Contents

# Introduction

For over 100 years, the term 'British cinema' has meant many different things to a range of interested parties. Notoriously, to François Truffaut, it was a nonsense term as he regarded 'British' and 'cinema' as incompatible. To financiers and sales agents, it is an industry, pure and simple, a world of high finance, tax breaks, budget sheets, mega-deals and the sales talk of Wardour Street film companies.

To academics, film students and auteurs, it is an art form, with key films lighting a cultural candle in a cynical, fast-food, Hollywood-dominated world.

To politicians it is a weapon used by successful governments to claim British cinema is alive and well (and that their policies for the arts are working) each year when someone British wins a Best Supporting Actor Oscar or when a film such as *Bean* (1997) makes tens of millions of dollars at the US and UK box office.

British cinema can be the internationalism of *Four Weddings and A Funeral* (1994) and *Notting Hill* (1999), and the regionalism of *Ratcatcher* (1999) and *Sweet Sixteen* (2002). It is Powell and Pressburger as well as *Kevin and Perry Go Large* (2000).

British cinema is all of these things, making it a fascinating national cinema to study, as it is also part of our lives and our history as well as part of our cultural heritage. It's important to realise that British cinema has a long and varied history, with a range of film styles that can stand against any country in the world, as well as writers, actors, directors and musicians that have enjoyed international acclaim, both with audiences and critics.

*'In effect, thanks entirely to the screen, the world is being taught to think in American...I have no wish to stop American films being shown in this country...but I am extremely anxious that British films shall also be seen. I do want to see British stories being produced by British firms...Have you not enough dramatic scenery and people in England, Ireland, Scotland and Wales to last us forever as subject matter?*

*Obviously we have, and therefore it only remains for us to be careful that our subject matter is true to the British temperament.'*

Eliot Stannard, screenwriter, in *Writing Screenplays* (undated but British Library sources say 1920) as quoted in *English Hitchcock* by Charles Barr [1]

In his notes to a recent Media Studies conference in Bradford, Robert Murphy talked of 'a need to overcome cultural prejudices' with regard to British cinema.[2]

This is true not only of audiences and critics outside the UK, but also for ourselves. As a nation we should learn to celebrate British cinema for itself, as a varied and vibrant national cinema, and see beyond the tabloid 'lottery funded movies lose money' dishonesty or the desperate race to keep up with Hollywood in terms of commercial success and domination of the world cinema markets.

Over the last few years, a new attitude has thankfully seen a more enlightened approach to British cinema, giving a range of films and film-makers the serious study they deserve, not only in terms of the film texts but analysis of the social, political and cultural contexts around them.

*Sight and Sound* thankfully is still around, with regular articles and reviews about British cinema. A new publication, *The Journal of British Cinema and Television* has just been launched and there are regular conferences and events around the country that specialise in discussions and screenings of British film. British and Irish cinema has finally been deemed worthy of study at A Level, with the introduction of the WJEC syllabus in 2000. In some ways, British cinema has never been so popular.

What I hope to do in this Guide is give an overview of recent British cinema, what themes and genres have been prevalent since the mid-1990s, look at the industry itself and also examine individual titles that hopefully will stimulate more discussion and therefore more viewing of British films in the classroom.

I intend this Guide and accompanying Classroom Resources to be fairly 'non academic' (a strange aim perhaps given the fact that I'm writing it for teachers and educationalists) but what I mean is that it should be used as a manual, a hands-on tool if you will[3] that will be useful to dip into as appropriate for anyone covering a range of topics around British cinema, in terms of the industry itself and the types of film it creates.

The key areas within this study are;

- **British cinema, past and present** – a brief history of British cinema from the end of the 19th century to 1990, its major themes and movements, and an extended section on British cinema of the 1990s to date, that is 2003.

- **Organisations and institutions** – an examination of the key bodies which fund our film industry and help to create our film culture, and also the mysterious world of production, distribution and exhibition, the last two areas being particularly obtuse to the general public.

- **Films in close-up** – case studies of five recent titles, with analysis of genre, narrative, representation and use of stars and how they work within the cultural and social context (i.e. *Trainspotting* (1996) as a Britpop movie, *Bridget Jones's Diary* (2001) as a product of Working Title Inc., *Sweet Sixteen* and the expression of working-class masculinity).

- **For further study** - information about further reading and viewing opportunities in the UK and some useful websites for further research, as well as a glossary of some frequently used terms in the film industry.

In my experience as Film Education Officer and later Film Programmer at the Tyneside Cinema in Newcastle Upon Tyne, many a teacher's requests began with 'Where can I find information on…', or 'Could you tell my students about what a distributor does?' (a question I often asked myself on many afternoons waiting for a film print to arrive for a show that evening). I therefore hope this pack will be useful as a 'one stop shop' of British cinema information for teachers of Film and Media Studies at both GCSE and A Level as well as other courses which specifically look at cinema in both a historical and cultural context.

Anyone using the WJEC Film Studies AS/A2 syllabus should also find the content a useful source, particularly as *Elizabeth* (1998) and *Sweet Sixteen* are both currently close study titles in FS3; and the work of such directors as Ken Loach, Gurinder Chadha and Danny Boyle could be used as interesting examples of British auteurs.

English teachers who use media and film in their work will also find it a useful introduction to some of the concepts and themes in cinema studies generally and may want to link it with any specific areas of Film Studies you may be working on (i.e. genre, auteur, national cinema, textual analysis).

Regarding the title of the guide, 'contemporary' will always be out of date and given the number of films released every week, it was impossible to keep up without changing my whole section on close study titles. What I have tried to do in that section is look at a range of titles from 1996 to 2002 that cover a number of different styles and genres along with some examples of films for further viewing up to 2004 that may complement the key film.

I have used two films to bookend the Close-Up section – *Trainspotting*, released in 1996 and *Bend It Like Beckham*, from 2002. I used those particular titles as they seem to represent the best that popular British cinema has to offer both the UK and the rest of the world. Both look at communities and cultures not normally seen in an international context (working class Scottish and English/Asian) and both seem to have latched onto the zeitgeist of their time perfectly. In the case of *Trainspotting*, it was the popularity of Britpop, and the rise in Scottish nationalism leading to a form of independence away from England. With *Bend It Like Beckham*, it was part of a move into the mainstream for Asian music, fashion and language, and also the peak of the David Beckham celebrity circus, climaxing in the 2002 World Cup and *that* toe.

Another thing both films have in common is the amazing financial success enjoyed both at home and abroad, given the relatively small budgets and difficult pitches: Scottish junkies take lots of heroin and Indian teenage girl wants to play football for Hounslow. *Trainspotting* cost around £1.74 million and took £12.4 million in the UK and over $16 million in the US; *Bend It Like Beckham* cost £2.7 million and took £11.4 million in the UK and over $32 million in the US to the end of 2003.[4]

Before going any further, it is perhaps useful to stop and think about what is meant by 'British cinema'.

# Defining British Cinema

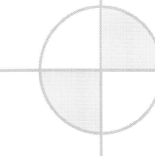

What do the following recently released films have in common?

*Buffalo Soldiers* (2001)
US soldiers get up to drug smuggling mischief on a German army base in the 1990s.

*L' Homme Du Train* (2002)
A French petty criminal meets an ageing schoolteacher and their lives merge.

*In the Cut* (2003)
Jane Campion directs and Meg Ryan stars in this noir-ish thriller set in New York where a serial killer has been outwitting the cops.

*Noi Albinoi* (2003)
Strangely wonderful tale about a Finnish albino boy who falls in love with a beautiful garage worker.

The answer is they are all considered 'British' within the current definition of the UK Film Council as they are co-productions with other countries and are added (as are dozens of other similar titles) to the UK box office each year as admissions for 'British' films. This immediately causes problems when we are thinking about what a British film is, as in audience's eyes, none of the above would be ever considered British in terms of content, location, setting, cast or crew.

To define 'British cinema' then, is an extremely complex matter. Even defining what 'British' means is problematic, as the country itself is made up of many regions, nations, principalities, provinces, counties, races, religions, languages and dialects. The constant influx of other cultures such as Chinese, Indian, Pakistan and Italian make it impossible to state what is 'typically' British without resorting to crude stereotypes.

In terms of cinema, there is no more a typical British film than there is a typical British accent, so we should really think of national *cinemas* rather than one definite type of film culture. Sarah Street describes our cinema as being 'inflected with a multitude of different connotations',[5] which is true for British cinema's past as well as its present.

However, there are some definitions we can use when talking of a 'British' film and it is worth keeping these in mind when discussing particular titles. The Department of Media Culture and Sport (DCMS) and the UK Film Council (UKFC) use economic criteria when defining a film as British – where the seed funding came from, who supplied the production and development money, how many British cast and crew are employed – leading to some rather bizarre titles being classed as British as in the examples stated above.

Just as bizarrely, a film like Ang Lee's *Sense and Sensibility* (1995) is classed as American even though its cast, its setting, its locations, its screenwriter and source material are British.

# The official definition

According to the DCMS there are currently, under law, two ways that a film may qualify as being called British, either by satisfying the international co-production agreement *or* by meeting the tests set by the Films Act 1985.

The Films Act tests are as follows:

- **The maker test** – the film must be produced by a company that is registered and centrally managed and controlled in the UK, in another state of the European Union or Economic area, or in a country with which the European Community has assigned an Association Agreement.

- **The production cost test** – 70 per cent of the production costs of the film must be spent on film-making activity in the UK.

- **The labour cost test** – 70 per cent of the total production cost and 75 per cent of the total labour costs must have been paid to citizens or residents of the Commonwealth, EU or a country with an agreement with the European community. In both of the cases, the costs of two crew members and one actor who are *not* EU/Commonwealth must be deducted from the total.

- **Previously filmed material** – no more than 10 per cent of the running time of the film should be of a previously certificated film or from a film by a different maker (i.e. use of archive material, news footage, clips from previous movies, etc.).

In terms of the co-productions, the producers from each participating country must raise agreed shares of production costs and seek benefits from their own country to assist with the film.

The British Council, the government office which seeks to raise the profile of the UK overseas, has another set of criteria with which to delegate British status on a film. A film can be classed as British if it meets three of the following criteria:

*The list opposite shows the dominance of Hollywood blockbuster titles at the UK box office. Entertainment is the only UK independent film distributor mentioned and even they have a releasing agreement with US studio New Line, hence titles such as* Lord of the Rings *(2001-3) in their library.*

*The only three films that can conceivably be called British in terms of their cultural content, narrative and personnel –* Love Actually *(2003),* Johnny English *(2003) and* Calendar Girls *(2003) – were all co-funded and released by American studios.*

1) It has a British producer.

2) It has a British production team (i.e. producers, editors, composers, writers, etc.).

3) It has a British director.

4) It has a predominantly British cast.

5) It has a subject matter that informs the British experience.

6) It has a British identity as defined by *Sight and Sound* magazine in the review section.

The other major problem with defining a 'British' film is that in the main, British cinema has meant *English* cinema, in terms of language and setting. Scotland, Wales and Northern Ireland all have their own funding bodies and Film Development organisations and a number of diverse and innovative films have been produced there. It is important therefore to consider films such as *Ratcatcher, Titanic Town* (1998) and *Twin Town* (1997) as very much productions of their home nations rather than just 'British' films.

The British Film Institute's Information Unit also has a series of classifications that it uses when discussing British films, and it is useful to take that system as general guide. The classifications take into consideration the *cultural* dimension of the film (that is, how it represents British life and society) as well as how the film was financed.

The five categories are shown below, with a brief explanation of criteria and some examples of recent titles. All refer to feature films (i.e. longer than 72 minutes).

### CATEGORY A
The cultural and financial input has been generated from the UK and the majority of the cast and crew are British. Examples: *Morvern Callar* (2002); *Anita and Me* (2002); *Purely Belter* (2000).

# Figure 1 The top 30 Films at UK box office 2003

| 1 | Finding Nemo * | Buena Vista Int. UK | £37,305,425 |
|---|---|---|---|
| 2 | The Lord of the Rings: Return of the King * | Entertainment | £35,344,979 |
| 3 | The Matrix: Reloaded | Warner Bros | £33,292,898 |
| 4 | Love Actually * | UIP | £30,824,521 |
| 5 | Pirates of the Caribbean: Curse of the Black Pearl | Buena Vista Int. UK | £28,171,721 |
| 6 | The Lord of the Rings: The Two Towers | Entertainment | £24,970,872 |
| 7 | Bruce Almighty | Buena Vista Int. UK | £23,642,290 |
| 8 | X-Men 2 | 20th Century Fox | £20,604,154 |
| 9 | Calendar Girls * | Buena Vista Int. UK | £20,330,070 |
| 10 | Johnny English | UIP | £19,634,179 |
| 11 | Terminator 3: Rise of the Machines | Columbia TriStar | £18,909,904 |
| 12 | The Matrix: Revolutions | Warner Bros | £17,798,650 |
| 13 | American Pie: The Wedding | UIP | £17,011,925 |
| 14 | Chicago | Buena Vista Int. UK | £16,229,017 (excludes 2002 grosses) |
| 15 | Elf | Entertainment | £15,256,315 |
| 16 | Catch Me If You Can | UIP | £15,065,226 |
| 17 | Two Weeks' Notice | Warner Bros | £13,524,795 |
| 18 | 8 Mile | UIP | £13,254,845 |
| 19 | Charlie's Angels: Full Throttle | Columbia TriStar | £12,355,642 |
| 20 | Kill Bill: Vol.1 | Buena Vista Int. UK | £11,535,333 |
| 21 | Gangs of New York | Entertainment | £10,563,616 |
| 22 | The Ring | UIP | £9,675,766 |
| 23 | Bad Boys II | Columbia TriStar | £8,686,047 |
| 24 | The Hulk | UIP | £8,364,049 |
| 25 | The Jungle Book 2 | Buena Vista Int. UK | £8,276,027 |
| 26 | Maid in Manhattan | Columbia TriStar | £8,240,828 |
| 27 | The Italian Job | UIP | £7,713,411 |
| 28 | 2 Fast 2 Furious | UIP | £7,570,861 |
| 29 | The League of Extraordinary Gentlemen | 20th Century Fox | £7,358,166 |
| 30 | Spy Kids 3D: Game Over | Buena Vista Int. UK | £7,259,036 |

* Film still on release when the data was compiled. Source: Film Distributors Association

## CATEGORY B

Co-productions where the majority of the finance and personnel are British and there is a strong British cultural content.
Examples: *Regeneration* (1997); *Bloody Sunday* (2002); *The Land Girls* (1998).

## CATEGORY C

Co-productions where the majority of financial input and cultural content is non-UK. However, the foreign involvement is not from the USA.
Examples: *Deathwatch* (2002); *Intimacy* (2001); *Ordinary Decent Criminal* (2000).

## CATAGORY D

American financed (or partly financed) films mainly shot in the UK. Most titles have UK cultural content.
Examples: *102 Dalmatians* (2000); *Bridget Jones's Diary*; *Saving Private Ryan* (1998).

## CATEGORY E

Mainly American films with some UK financial involvement and, in some cases, a small number of British cast or crew but may have little or no UK cultural content in terms of setting or story.
Examples: *The Big Lebowski* (1998); *Evita* (1996); *Romeo is Bleeding* (1993).

It is plain by the above definitions, that what constitutes a 'British' film is more complex than just where it was produced or who the stars are. However, in the audience's eyes, it is essentially cultural and nationality issues that make a British film, such as setting, location of filming, original source material, main cast, and possibly director or scriptwriter. So to the general public, *Cold Mountain* (2003) is American and *Sense and Sensibility* is British, even though technically they are both US/UK co-productions.

Finally, on the subject of definitions, I think it is useful to consider three separate areas when thinking about the idea of British cinema:

- **'The British film industry'** –

That is, the economic and financial model, which includes the production, distribution and exhibition sectors, where the main concern is creating a profitable, commercial, internationally successful business which will generate income through the box office and related areas (merchandising, video and DVD sales, TV rights, etc.).

- **'British cinema'** –

The study of British films and their history, through actual texts, and also the social, cultural and historical contexts around them, mainly through formal and informal studies, education work and publications.

- **'British film culture'** –

This does not just relate to producing and watching *British* films. To have a healthy film culture in the UK we should have an international dimension in terms of our film viewing. Watching and learning about World cinema, in cinemas, on television and on video or DVD, should be encouraged and should be an integral part of our formal and informal cultural experience.

There are obviously overlaps in these definitions, and it would be naïve to expect either to exist in a vacuum without any need of the other. For example, the small number of foreign language films we see on UK screens is directly linked to the economic realities of distribution, exhibition and retail as is the comparatively high cost of foreign films and silent cinema on DVD and video.[6]

However, the danger is that the industrial/economic model will dominate at the expense of the artistic and the cultural, so it is vital for a vibrant and healthy British film culture that these areas are balanced. A definition of success and how 'good' a film is cannot be judged on worldwide box office income alone.

# A Brief History of British Cinema

## Silent Days (1895–1929)

Before World War I, Britain along with other European countries such as France, Germany and Sweden actually dominated the world in terms of producing films and film-makers. Indeed, before the acknowledged date of the invention of cinema, December 1895, when the Lumière Brothers first screened a moving picture film before a paying audience, a number of British innovators had experimented with photographic and mechanical motion picture machines.

Birt Acres filmed the Derby and the Oxford–Cambridge Boat race in 1895, Louis Le Prince filmed traffic in Leeds in the late 1880s and Wordsworth Donisthrorpe (a truly wonderful English name that surely belongs in an Ealing comedy) filmed a view of Trafalgar Square in 1890. Their trouble was they could not combine recording images with a camera *and* projecting those images on `to a screen.

These heroic individuals who just missed out as being recognised as inventing the greatest art form of the last two centuries could be a metaphor for British cinema itself. Inventive, artistic, creative, but thought of as second to Hollywood in terms of popularity and international money-making appeal and also perceived as not being as 'arty' as the true art cinema of Europe. However these early pioneers in British cinema can certainly stand alongside other world film-makers with their innovative work.

Robert Paul used the close-up in *The Twins Tea Party* (1897) and A.G. Smith went further with the extreme close-up in *Grandma's Reading Glass* (1900). James Williamson brought the tracking shot to the screen with *The Big Swallow* (1901) and used colour tinting and early editing techniques in *Fire!* the same year. But it was Cecil Hepworth who became the first true artist of British cinema, using a range of styles and innovative techniques that far out stripped his rivals. His version of *Alice in Wonderland* (1903) was almost 10 minutes long and linked 16 different scenes using dissolves. His most famous film, *Rescued by Rover* (1905), was way ahead of other films of the time in its use of editing and camera movement (including panning shots and low angle shots) to move along the narrative.

Classics of literature provided a rich mine for film-makers to dig with adaptations of the work of Charles Dickens and Shakespeare being the most popular. During and after World War I, a combination of American dominance and government taxes on entertainment and leisure activities affected business, and by 1925 only 5 per cent of films shown in the UK were British made. However, a group of young, cultured producers, writers and directors came together not only to create films - hits at the time included *Alf's Button* (1921), *Squibs* (1921) and *Woman to Woman* (1923) – but also to form The London Film Society, where films from across the world were given screenings. Films such as *Battleship Potemkin* (1925) and *The Cabinet of Dr Caligari* (1919) were seen and in turn influenced the work of British artists.

Among the film-makers who started their careers at this time were Alfred Hitchcock, Herbert Wilcox and Michael Balcon, all of whom found varying degrees of success over the next four decades. Hitchcock proved to be the most innovative and controversial of the group, releasing *The Lodger* (1926), with its imaginative use of visuals to portray the inner thoughts of its characters, and *Blackmail* (1929), acknowledged as the first British all-talking film.

# Golden Years (1930–1960)

With the coming of sound, there also came international success for the British film industry. Alfred Hitchcock continued his run of entertaining and enthralling thrillers including *The Man Who Knew Too Much* (1934), *The 39 Steps* (1935) and *The Lady Vanishes* (1938) and producers such as Victor Saville and Herbert Wilcox also had success, particularly with costume dramas, literary classics and historical epics such as *The Good Companions* (1933), *Nell Gwynne* (1934) and *Victoria the Great* (1937). However, the most successful entrepreneur who sold the British image abroad proved to be a Hungarian immigrant called Alexander Korda. His film (which he also directed), *The Private Life of Henry VIII* (1933), was a huge international success, winning a Best Actor Oscar for Charles Laughton and setting off a mini-cycle of entertaining (and historically hilarious) biopics such as *Catherine the Great* (1934) and *Rhodes Of Africa* (1936).

The stars that were beginning to shine included Robert Donat, Michael Redgrave and Anna Negal, but the most popular proved to be a young music hall singer from Rochdale called Gracie Fields, who dominated the box office with a series of cheery musicals, where a working-class lass triumphs over adversity and big business. By 1937, she was the highest paid film star in the world.

The documentary movement, begun in earnest by John Grierson in the early 1930s, gave thousands of working-class citizens a previously unheard voice against the

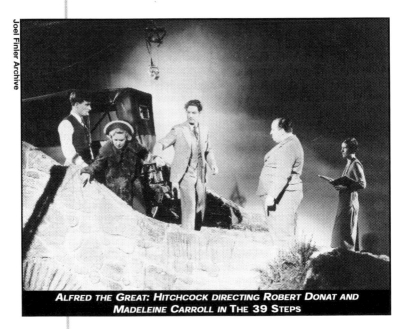

**ALFRED THE GREAT: HITCHCOCK DIRECTING ROBERT DONAT AND MADELEINE CARROLL IN THE 39 STEPS**

poverty and exploitation of their lives and showed their contribution to Britain's industrial wealth. *Housing Problems* (1935), *Night Mail* (1936) and *Coal Face* (1936) are perhaps the best known and the movement continued through World War II with a mixture of propaganda and public information films such as *Listen To Britain* (1941), *Fires Were Started* (1943) and *Western Approaches* (1944).

During World War II, cinemagoers were given not only the obvious propaganda films (*Went the Day Well?* (1942), Leslie's Howard's *The First of the Few* (1942) and *The Way Ahead* (1944)), but also some welcome escapism from the conflict. Gainsborough Pictures produced a series of colourful costume dramas, showing off a range of new stars, mostly graduates from the Rank charm school. Margaret Lockwood, Stewart Granger, James Mason and Phyllis Calvert bounded through such films as *The Wicked Lady* (1945) and *The Man in Grey* (1943) and by 1946 annual admissions were at an all time high of 1,635 million, a figure that has yet to be beaten.

A partnership which began in the 1930s and flourished throughout the 40s and 50s was between man of Kent Michael Powell and Hungarian immigrant Emeric Pressburger. This unlikely pairing produced some of British cinema's most memorable and original works including *The Life and Death of Colonel Blimp* (1943), *A Canterbury Tale* (1944), *A Matter of Life and Death* (1946), *The Red Shoes* (1948) and *The Tales of Hoffmann* (1951).

A cycle of films which also gained both critical and public acclaim were the comedies produced by Ealing Studios, with a stock company of stars and directors. The bias towards the 'little man' fighting against authority and the pompous and suspicious bureaucrats seen to get their come-uppance proved a welcome relief from post-war rationing and national austerity. *The Ladykillers* (1955) and *Kind Hearts and Coronets* (1949) were perhaps the blackest, with murder and greed the central themes, but just as original were *Whiskey Galore!* (1949) and *Passport to Pimlico* (1949).

The 1950s saw a steady decline in audiences but a range of international co-productions, particularly with America, which saw successes such as *The African Queen* (1952), David Lean's epic *The Bridge on the River Kwai* (1957) and *Captain Horatio Hornblower* (1952), all with Hollywood stars.

However, two of the most successful film series which began in the 1950s relied solely on very British strands of popular culture – bawdy humour that stars like George Formby had first found an audience with; and the gothic horror tradition that went back to British writers such as Robert Louis Stevenson, Mary Shelly and M.R. James.

Both the *Carry On...* series and the horror productions of the Hammer Studios have much in common. Both began in the late 1950s, continuing into the 1970s. Both were generally dismissed by critics but loved by audiences and both have seen a comeback of sorts over the last decade, with articles, books and seminars reappraising their place in the canon of British cinema. Certainly, each series has produced classics of their kind. Terence Fisher's initial *Frankenstein* and *Dracula* adaptations (1957 and 1958, respectively) and the gloriously original (and extremely camp) *Dr Jekyll and Sister Hyde* (1971), have become part of the classic horror genre, and the best of *Carry On*'s film parodies were spot on, namely *Carry On Spying* (1964), *Carry On Cleo* (1964) and *Carry On, Don't Lose Your Head* (1967). The two genres even came together in a bizarre combination, *Carry On Screaming* (1966) with Kenneth Williams most memorable as the deranged Dr Watt (itself a take on the BBC's cult new series, *Dr Who*).

# New Directions (1958–1970)

Frustrated with the direction of British cinema in the mid-1950s, a group of young critics and film-makers including Tony Richardson and Lindsay Anderson, challenged the mainstream initially with a series of written statements in a manifesto distributed at a programme of short films screened at the National Film Theatre in London in February 1956. The programme was called 'Free Cinema', and the demands laid out in programme note were not unlike the Dogme manifesto from Sweden 40 years later, for example:

> *'Perfection is not an aim…the image speaks…no film can be too personal…a style means an attitude…an attitude means a style'.*

Those film-makers, and others, moved into features and the British New Wave was born. The films sought to distance the film-makers from the prevalent style and content of British films at the time (middle-class, no challenging artistic modes, no voice for the young and articulate generation). The movement became known as Free Cinema and the film-makers, including Anderson,

Richardson and Karel Reisz, adapted stories from the theatre and the literature of the time including *Room at the Top* (1958), *Look Back in Anger* (1959), *A Taste of Honey* (1960), *Saturday Night and Sunday Morning* (1960) and *The Loneliness of the Long Distance Runner* (1962).

*REGIONAL REALISM: BRITISH CINEMA MOVES FORWARD WITH CLASSICS SUCH AS THE LONELINESS OF THE LONG DISTANCE RUNNER*

The films had a number of key elements that made them unique at the time – portrayal of the English working-class as an articulate group rather than painful comic relief, regional settings and locations, a realist style, frankness around sex and sexuality – and they proved themselves at the UK box office and with international audiences.

As the decade went on, a new audience appeared: the teenager. Financially independent, educated and sexually confident, film-makers were initially slow to capture their world, but films such as *A Hard Day's Night* (1964), *Smashing Time* (1967), *Georgy Girl* (1966) and *Blow Up* (1966) at last attempted to capture the world of Swinging London and the burgeoning pop culture that was being created around it. More discerning films describing the temper of the times appeared by the end of the decade, reflecting the revolutionary spirit of the young audience, now politically motivated and taking their music and culture seriously – *If...*(1968), *Bronco Bullfrog* (1969), *Privilege* (1967) and *Performance* (1970).[7]

# Fall and ... Fall (1970–1984)

By 1970, even with the introduction of a new Film Act, which kept the British Quota at 30 per cent and increased funding to the Film Finance Corporation, audiences were still decreasing[8] and the number of British films being produced was slowing down. A series of Hollywood disaster movies just about kept audiences in cinemas and the majority of successful titles were co-produced with the United States such as the continuing James Bond series, and inflated all star epics such as *A Bridge Too Far* (1977), *Superman 2* (1981) and *Death On the Nile* (1978).

There were stirrings of an independent British spirit, particularly in the experimental or 'art house' sector – Peter Greenaway and Derek Jarman began working on features in the early 1980s – and there were certainly some British films produced at this time that have become classics such as *Get Carter* (1971), *Don't Look Now* (1973), *The Wicker Man* (1973) and *The Long Good Friday* (1980) but it seemed that Britain as a vital world film force was dead. UK productions by 1980 had fallen to 38 and in the same year, Rank, a company that had become an icon for British cinema with its famous gong logo, announced it was ending film production.

There seemed to be hope in early 1982 when *Chariots of Fire* (1981) won 4 Oscars including Best Film and Colin Welland made his now infamous echo of Paul Revere at the podium, 'the British are coming!'. But as cinema admissions continued to fall (an all time low in 1984 at 54 million) and with the advent of home video recorders

(3.2 million VCR machines in the UK by 1983), it seemed that both production and exhibition would never recover.

# Changing Fortunes (1984-1996)

The 1980s and early 1990s saw a revival of both the cultural and economic fortunes of British cinema, and laid a foundation of production values, a visual aesthetic and a thankfully fluid definition of what British culture means that continues to this day.

Perhaps the desperate days of 1984 with the lowest annual cinema admissions ever recorded in the UK proved that the only way was up and resurgence began almost immediately with regard to admissions, mainly due to the arrival of a bright shiny American import...the multiplex.

The UK's first multiplex was The Point, opened by American corporation AMC in November 1985 in Milton Keynes and soon audiences began to rise, enthralled by this new gleaming cinema experience. Multiplexes were a world away from the dingy, slightly seedy feel of a lot of high street cinemas and they had the latest sound technology, a huge array of sweets and drinks (or 'concessions' as they are known in multi-speak), between 10–15 screens, lots of parking and up to 5 or 6 screenings a day of each title.

In terms of film production, one of the major players in the UK production sector during the 1980s and 1990s proved to be Channel Four, which provided backing to a number of films that have proved the test of time, including *Angel* (1982), *The Draughtsman's Contract* (1982), *The Company of Wolves* (1984) and *Dance with a Stranger* (1986).

George Harrison's company Handmade Films also proved itself in the film arena with a series of witty and original films such as *Withnail and I* (1986), *Monty Python's Life Of Brian* (1979) and *A Private Function* (1984). Another vibrant young company, Palace Pictures appeared on the scene in the early 80s with titles such as, *Scandal* (1988) and *Letter to Brezhnev* (1984).

A new strand of independent art cinema began to gain popularity, with directors like Peter Greenaway, Derek Jarman, Terence Davies and Sally Potter all producing a range of innovative and challenging work that allowed British cinema to be judged as an artistic and cultural force, rather than simply desperately trying to beat Hollywood at its own game at the box office.

One particular genre rose to great prominence during the 1980s and beyond, and became almost synonymous with British cinema itself, certainly in the USA: the costume drama. Typified by a successful series of Merchant/Ivory titles such as *A Room with a View* (1984), and *Maurice* (1987) the films were attacked by some critics for their seemingly unquestioning acceptance of the upper-class and aristocratic values they portrayed.

British cinema had always had this type of film – the Gainsborough melodramas from the 1940s and a host of adaptations of Shakespeare and English literature classics since the 1930s – but it wasn't until the 1990s that critical debate around the genre's content and style widened. Critics replaced the phrase 'costume drama' with 'heritage film', a slightly dismissive description which has caused debate in critical and academic circles, where it first appeared in the late 1980s and early 1990s, for its pejorative connotations.

Although the 1980s and early 1990s were dominated politically and socially by the harsh economic policies of Thatcherism, cinema seemed to rise to the challenge, with a series of defiant political works giving voice to the working class such as Ken Loach's *Hidden Agenda* (1990), *Riff Raff* (1992) and *Raining Stones* (1993), Mike

**A ROOM WITH A VIEW: A RARE INTERNATIONAL SUCCESS FOR BRITISH CINEMA IN THE 1980S**

Leigh's *Naked* (1992) and the slightly more audience-friendly *Brassed Off* (1995).

By the mid-1990s, *Four Weddings and a Funeral* had become the yardstick with which to measure success in British cinema with its massive box office take both here and in the USA. However, along with Kenneth Branagh's Shakespearian adaptations and the Merchant/Ivory classic costume dramas, *Four Weddings...* could be said to inhabit the world of the Edwardian heritage film in terms of its plot and content (social and romantic complications of the Southern upper middle-classes, set against a background of country hotels, stately homes and castles) even if it did have a contemporary 90s setting.

Then, on the same day in February 1996, two films were released that showed with almost surreal synchronicity the two main directions that the British national cinema would take – one was a sumptuous version of a Jane Austen novel about love, hidden passions and the English reserve, starring Emma Thompson, Kate Winslet,

Alan Rickman, Greg Wise and Hugh Grant, called *Sense and Sensibility*. The other was a scorching adaptation of Irvine Welsh's novel about heroin, drink and the Scot's hatred of the English and themselves, starring Ewan McGregor, Robert Carlyle, Ewen Bremner, Jonny Lee Miller and Kelly McDonald – *Trainspotting*.

# Britpop, Brit.lit and Brit.grit: Aspects of British Cinema from 1996

Through the 1990s and up to the present day there has again been a roller coaster ride for British cinema with huge international box office successes being set against an increasingly competitive financial world for independent and cultural producers, distributors and exhibitors.

During the late nineties and early years of the 21st century, the traditional themes and genres prevalent in British cinema over the last century are still there, but many have been given new dimensions and twists. For example, the costume drama, that staple of middle-class, middle-England cinema, is now the 'heritage film' and recent titles have moved away from merely portraying Victorian and Edwardian aristocracy at home and abroad, but have reflected elements of contemporary society (class conflict, the role of women) and tried to capture the youth market of Hollywood blockbusters. An example of this (though not particularly successful at the box office) was *Plunkett and Mclean* (1999), a bawdy tale of two 18th century highwaymen, which attempted to combine the attitude of *Trainspotting*, the mise-en-scène of a Gainsborough

melodrama and the script of a *Carry On...* film. The
presence of two *Trainspotting* stars in the lead roles (Robert
Carlyle and Jonny Lee Miller), the backing of Working Title
as a production partner and a knowing sense of humour
(the poster's tagline was *'They rob the rich…that's it!'*)
wasn't enough to make it a hit (£2.7 million at the UK
box office against a budget of £10 million).

*Trainspotting* did seem to give British cinema a shot in the
arm (so to speak) and help enhance its international profile,
not only against the more traditional British genres (costume
dramas, social realism) but to show that film from this
country could be a vibrant, exciting stylistic cinema that
wasn't afraid to market itself to international audiences.

© Columbia TriStar

© Universal Video

**THE FILMS NOW ARRIVING...TWO 'BRITISH' FILMS, BOTH RELEASED
ON THE SAME DAY IN FEBRUARY 1996, STRIVING FOR TWO VERY
DIFFERENT AUDIENCES AT THE BOX OFFICE**

As an influence on youth cinema, *Trainspotting* had an
immediate affect, with the inevitable comparisons used
by other films in their marketing campaigns, such as
*Twin Town* (1996) and *The Acid House* (1998), which was
also based on stories by Irvine Welsh and starring
*Trainspotting* alumni Ewen Bremner and Kevin McKidd.

*Twin Town* shares a number of elements with *Trainspotting* – non-English setting, the uncompromising sex and drugs lifestyle of young working-class males, the dark humour, the non-tourist portrayal of a major town, in this case Swansea ('a pretty shitty city' to quote the film, a response to Dylan Thomas' description of the city) – and also plays on Welsh stereotypes the same way *Trainspotting* does with Scottish ones. The opening monologue can be compared with Renton's rant against consumerism and his blast against the Scots themselves:

> *'Rugby. Tom Jones. Male voice choirs. Shirley Bassey. Prince of Wales. Daffodils. Sheep shaggers. Coal. Now if that's your idea of Welsh culture, you can't blame us for trying to liven the place up a bit, can you?'*

Another interesting film usually classed as being in the tradition of *Trainspotting* is *Boston Kickout* (1995), written and directed by Paul Hills, set in the bleak townscape of Stevenage. *Empire* magazine described it as 'the snotty nosed kid brother to *Trainspotting*' but although it was released in October 1996, 8 months after *Trainspotting* it was conceived and shot in 1994/1995 and premiered in the USA in October 1995. The teenagers portrayed in *Boston Kickout* have similar lives to Renton et al (boredom, lack of opportunities, problems with a violent sociopath in the Begbie mould) but director Hills gives the film a style and an energy that deserves to see it break away from its *Trainspotting* shadow.

It also has a cast of (then) unknowns that are now some of the new generation of British cinema and television actors, including John Simm (*The Lakes, State of Play*), Andrew Lincoln (*Teachers, This Life*) and Marc Warren (*Hustle*).

*Human Traffic* (1999) continued the *Trainspotting* tradition of mixing 90s club culture and music, a disparate bunch of teens and twenty-somethings indulging in sex and drugs and a mixture of realism/surrealism side by side. The film followed an acclaimed BBC TV film, *Loved Up* starring Lena Heady and Ian Hart (and also Danny Dyer who starred in *Human Traffic*).

*Human Traffic* hasn't aged well as the 'loved-up' language and characters seem very dated – it was filmed in 1998 and released in June 1999 – but it does capture the excitement and sheer noise of the late 90s UK club scene and has an excellent young cast, particularly John Simm and Danny Dyer as the paranoid Moff, swinging from high ecstasy to deep depression. It also has a sharp dig at the tabloid coverage of the drug and club culture in the scene where a BBC documentary crew stops Lulu and Nina in a club to talk to 'real' clubbers. The girls say they don't take ecstasy just heroin – 'we never used to but then we saw *Trainspotting* and they just made us want to do it'.

*South West 9* (2001), set in and around Brixton, also sets out to show the hip and happening London club 'n' drug scene ('*no ordinary day trip*' is the poster tag line) with a myriad of characters seen over 24 hours in a number of escapades. Flirting with anti-capitalist protests (The Levellers appear in a cameo role) as well as the club scene, *SW9* covers a wider base than *Human Traffic* but the emphasis is concentrated on portraying the London young as hip and happening drug takers and ravers.

During the 1990s and early 2000s, it wasn't just the youth film that seemed to be going through a metamorphosis. Traditional genres such as comedy, social realism and the costume drama began to evolve and hybrids were formed, proving highly successful both in the UK and abroad. The social realist drama, once the domain of only one or two film-makers such as Ken Loach and Mike Leigh, began to flower with young directors such as Shane Meadows exploring the world outside London (Nottingham rather the Notting Hill) with highly personal portraits of young working-class protagonists set in the East Midlands beginning with the low budget *TwentyFourSeven* (1997) and *A Room For Romeo Brass* (1998) (costing £4.5 million between them) with unknowns and non-professional actors, and then a (relatively) all star cast *Once Upon A Time In the Midlands* (2002), costing £3 million.

With reference to the cycle of social realist dramas at this time, 'the working underclass' is a phrase developed from a description used by American academic Charles Murray in *The Emerging British Underclass*, which according to Claire Monk sought to 'portray(ing) a class seen as parasitically dependent and work-shy rather than work-less'.[10]

Monk goes on to look at a series of films that, in continuing the work of the British New Wave and the films of Ken Loach and Mike Leigh during the 1980s and 80s, show a series of working class (mainly) males in situations where their guile, a canniness and earthy humour, and sometimes a dangerous veer towards the criminal, help to alleviate the fact that they are unemployed, disenfranchised by society, lacking in education, social status and wealth.

Two films in particular, released within a year of each other and usually spoken and written about in these terms. *The Full Monty* (1997) and *Brassed Off* (1996) are on the surface very similar, but they also have elements that set them apart.

Released nine months apart, the two films have obvious similarities. They were both sold as comedies, with *Brassed Off* having an additional romantic element through the relationship between Gloria (a good old-fashioned 'northern' name) and Andy. Both were set in Yorkshire and based round traditional industries (mining and steelworking). Both attacked the Thatcherite policies of the Conservative government and both showed a group of men trying to find ways out of their predicament – one traditional (using brass band music), one 'unnatural' (male stripping).

*The Full Monty* is played mainly for laughs with a mixture of visual gags and jokes, *Carry On*-type innuendo and a number of comedy set pieces, most famously the dole queue dance to Donna Summers' *Hot Stuff*. *Brassed Off*, although containing amusing sequences and dialogue, is much darker in tone and is a much more political film in the sense that blame is given out to the (then current) Tory government directly, first by Phil (Stephen Tompkinson) as he's having a breakdown at a children's party, and then in the impassioned final speech by the dying Danny (Pete Postlethwaite) at the band concert in the Albert Hall.

*TRAGIC COMEDY:* BRASSED OFF LOOKS AT POLITICS, DEATH, LOSS OF DIGNITY, INDUSTRIAL DECAY AND ATTEMPTED SUICIDE

Significantly this speech takes place in the centre of London, the centre of the film world as well as the political and commercial world in the UK, and could be seen as throwing London's metro-centred culture of *Four Weddings/Notting Hill/Bridget Jones/Love Actually* back in its face.

Not as successful *The Full Monty* in box office success,[11] *Brassed Off* is actually a much more interesting film in terms of themes and content than its romcom marketing image sets it up to be, and is certainly worth closer examination.[12]

Regionalism became *the* thing in British cinema features during the 1990s, with locations across Britain being used as 'the real thing' rather than just backdrops to pad out footage between London based sequences. Apart from Grimethorpe, Halifax (*Brassed Off*) and Sheffield (*The Full Monty*) we have been treated to big screen views of Newcastle Upon Tyne (*Purely Belter, Gabriel and Me* (2000) and *The One And Only* (2001)), East Durham (*Billy Elliot* (1999)), Manchester (*24 Hour Party People* (2001)) and Cardiff (*Human Traffic*).

There was also a rise in new talent coming from the regions including the aforementioned Shane Meadows from Nottingham, Lynne Ramsay from Glasgow, and Michael Winterbottom from Manchester, who have all made a mark on the national and international scene, but have also kept their local perspective, making films either in their region or about local subjects.

Perhaps the most recent successful British genre internationally (apart from the USA co-production franchise of James Bond and the Harry Potter series) has been comedy, particularly the films produced by the Working Title Company. Based in London, and co-funded by Universal Studios in Hollywood and StudioCanal in France, they have international distribution deals for their films across Europe, US and other key territories, so before the film is even made, it is 'booked' into screens across the world. This is obviously a massive plus in creating an audience for the films and has helped them build a worldwide box office of over 2.5 *billion* dollars.

Following on from *Four Weddings and a Funeral* there was the 'Hugh Grant + a Hollywood actress to attract the US audience' series of *Notting Hill, Bridget Jones's Diary* and *Love Actually*, all which proved hugely popular at the UK and international box office. In the US and UK to date (April 2004) these four films *alone* have taken at least $501,000,000 (that's around £333,000,000).[13] For the USA and the rest of the world then, with a few international exceptions (*Billy Elliot, The Full Monty*), British cinema *is* Working Title and London based romantic comedy. *Sliding Doors* (1997) was not a Working Title picture but had a *Four Weddings...* connection in the casting of John Hannah, and also had a bankable US star (Gwyneth Paltrow) playing a London girl, complete with a (rather good, in fact) estuary accent.

One of the interesting aspects of *Sliding Doors* was its rather tragic denouement (for one of Paltrow's characters at least) which comes as a shock to the audience, but fits perfectly with the randomness of the 'what could have happened if...' plotline.

*Bedrooms and Hallways* (1997) and *This Year's Love* (1999), two ensemble 'La Ronde' comedies of cosmopolitan twenty/thirty somethings looking for love by sleeping with and leaving various different partners, were also based in the capital and featured a host of recognisable stars from British film and TV including Jennifer Ehle, Kathy Burke, Kevin McKidd and Dougray Scott.

*This Year's Love* in particular had an almost tragic air about it, separating it from the usual romcom fare, with David Gray's maudlin but affecting soundtrack, Ian Hart as the mentally unstable Liam and the wonderful final sequence with Kathy Burke singing her lonely karaoke song, a heartbroken but unbowed woman.

At the time of writing, *Love Actually* is the latest international hit from the Working Title stable, but there is also an up and coming generation of writers and directors, brought up on 1990s TV comedy such as *Vic Reeves Big Night Out* and *The Fast Show* that will hopefully refresh the genre. The most recent has been *Shaun of the Dead* (2004) the critically acclaimed film debut from Simon Pegg and Edgar Wright, creators of the *Spaced* TV series, which took over £4,000,000 at the UK box office in its first two weeks.

The other major British genre that continues to dominate the national and international box office is the aforementioned heritage film. The suspicion lingered that the films continued to uphold the dominant attitudes of the aristocracy (and by inference the then current Conservative government) by showing the gardens, great houses, costumes and manners of the rich without any reference to the 'ordinary' classes.

However, a closer examination of films such as Merchant-Ivory's *Howard's End* (1992) and *The Remains of the Day* (1993) and Iain Softley's adaptation of Henry James' *The Wings of the Dove* (1997) show that the upper classes are represented as greedy and selfish, and not paragons of an idealised English lifestyle. This harshness of style and content refreshed the genre, and there were some rich and original works released during this time, with Jane Austen in particularly getting rather a drastic make-over. Emma Thompson's emotional adaptation of *Sense and Sensibility* was a witty and warm version of the story, and as directed by Ang Lee, had a rich visual texture. *Mansfield Park* (1999), directed by Patricia Rozema, brought a violence and a sexuality to the surface that had hitherto been hidden in Austen's work and Roger Michell's made-for-TV *Persuasion* proved a subtle and low key addition to the canon when it was released into cinemas in 1996.

MANSFIELD PARK

FOR EVERYONE WHO LOVED "EMMA" AND "SENSE & SENSIBILITY" COMES THE STORY JANE AUSTEN LOVED BEST.

DVD

**AUSTEN'S POWER: ADAPTATIONS OF HER CLASSIC WORKS ACHIEVED VARYING DEGREES OF SUCCESS AT THE UK BOX OFFICE**

As well as plundering the literary canon, English history and the Royal Family were also used as source material with the best and most successful including *The Madness of King George* (1995) and *Mrs Brown* (1997), both of which could be taken as witty commentaries on the then-current problems of the Royal Family including press intrusions, love affairs and the role of the Prince of Wales. *Elizabeth* was sold as a political thriller and showed a glamorous young princess sacrificing love and happiness for her country and her duty – ironically just as the film's first scenes were being shot, news came from Paris that Princess Diana had been killed.

The most successful of the recent historical films was *Shakespeare in Love* (1999), again backed with Hollywood studio funding and distribution from Universal and Miramax and also with a major American star (Gwyneth Paltrow) in a lead role.

Another genre that had a brief resurgence in the late 1990s/early 2000s was the gangster film. Following in the wake of Guy Ritchie's surprise hit *Lock, Stock and Two Smoking Barrels* (1998), and influenced by British cult crime movies of the past such as *Get Carter* and *The Long Good Friday*, films such as *Essex Boys* (1999), *Rancid Aluminum* (2000) and Ritchie's own virtual remake, *Snatch* (2000) were soon forgotten by the public and the critics. The most memorable films proved to be *Gangster No. 1* (2000) with a powerhouse performance by Malcolm McDowell as the ageing king of the streets remembering how he used to be the 'guvnor', and the surreal *Sexy Beast* (2000), with Ray Winstone as the ex-con soaking up the sun in Spain, and Ben Kingsley (frighteningly psychotic) as the man sent to persuade him to do one last job.

Beginning in the mid-1980s, with films such as *My Beautiful Laundrette* (1985) and *Sammie and Rosie Get Laid* (1987), British Asian film-makers, writers and actors began to make a long-overdue headway into the British film industry. By the mid-1990s, people like Gurinder Chadha, Hanif Kureshi and Meera Syal were producing a range of films both mainstream and art house, giving very different perspectives on the Asian experience in modern Britain. Kureshi's political polemics such as *London Kills Me* (1991) and *My Son the Fanatic* (1997) reflected the anger and frustration of young Asians while Chadha's *Bhaji on the Beach* (1994) and *Bend It Like Beckham* examined to some extent the prejudices within the Asian community and the need for integration with other social and ethnic groups without losing identity.

Black (referring to cultures of Afro-Caribbean or African origin) film-makers were led in the main by Isaac Julien in the 1980s, with work such as *Looking for Langston* (1986), *Young Soul Rebels* (1992) and *Franz Fanon: White Skin Black Mask* (1997). However, due to lack of distribution and the relatively small scale of the release, these films never reached a mainstream audience.

*The Girl with Brains in her Feet* (1997), exploring the experiences of a black teenager growing up in early 1970s Leicester, and *Babymother* (1998) about a single mum trying to start a girl band (with yet another great tag line, *'From Ragga To Riches'* – yeah, go girl!) made some headway into the mainstream, but, unlike the music industry, Black and Asian voices haven't as yet permeated into the UK film industry to create a vibrant fusion of cultures.

There have also been some intriguing forays into non-mainstream experimental film that has produced some interesting and challenging work, following in the footsteps of Peter Greenaway and Derek Jarman. Greenaway himself ended the 1990s with *8 ½ Women* (1999) starring John Standing as a disillusioned businessman who heads off to Geneva in search of sexual treats. Greenaway stated that cinema had to reinvent itself and evolve to survive, and his latest work, *The Tulse Luper Suitcases* (2003) is a multi-media journey through images, text, music and sound with an amazing cast including Debbie Harry, Steven Macintosh, Victoria Abril, William Hurt and … Sting. If the official website is anything to go by, then the film is one of his masterworks, referencing art, history, the atomic bomb and Greenaway's own films. However, it seems to have proved too much for British cinema to bear as it has, as yet, not had a UK wide release.[14]

Patrick Keiller's *London* (1993) was a surreal trip around the capital, giving traditional images a new and anarchic sheen, for example linking the Lord Mayor's Show and Trooping of The Colour with the *ancien régime* during the French Revolution. In *Robinson in Space* (1997) Keiller expands his vision out of the city and across the country, exploring and deploring the state of Britain in a love/hate way – lovingly shooting stately homes and gardens while telling us their bloody history as oppressors of the unsung heroes of England and their links to their slave trade. *Gallivant* (1996) directed by Andrew Kötting, is another journey around Britain, this time with Kötting's daughter Eden and grandmother as our eyes and ears, as they experience a series of landscapes and people.

Some British film-makers have defied catagorisation as 'genre' directors. Michael Winterbottom has moved from costume drama (*Jude,* 1996), political docu-drama (*Welcome To Sarajevo*, 1997), film noir (*I Want You,* 1998), the western by way of Thomas Hardy's *Mayor of Casterbridge* (*The Claim*, 2000) and the retro-chic pop art film (*24 Hour Party People*, with it's classic poster tagline about Tony Wilson, king of Manchester's 80s club scene – *'Genius. Poet. Twat.'*).

Perhaps Winterbottom's greatest work is *Wonderland* (1999), a heart-breakingly beautiful film of love and despair, set in (for once) an unfriendly and unfeeling London, which doesn't care about its inhabitants at all.

FROM SUNDERLAND TO WONDERLAND... GINA MCKEE AS NADIA IN MICHAEL WINTERBOTTOM'S BEAUTIFUL BUT HARSH VISION OF LONDON IN WONDERLAND

Danny Boyle is another unclassifiable film-maker, constantly switching genres and styles from the lo-tech comedy thriller *Shallow Grave* (1994), the cult hit

*Trainspotting*, flawed attempts at the Hollywood mainstream with *A Life Less Ordinary* (1997) and *The Beach* (1999) and back on track with the zombie horror tale *28 Days Later* (2002).

There has been a wealth of young creative acting talent that has hit British screens, coming both from stage and television, some of which have moved across the Atlantic and made their mark in Hollywood, including Ewan McGregor, Samantha Morton, Kate Winslet, Keira Knightly, Rachel Weiz, Ian Hart, Emily Watson and Kate Beckinsale.

The current breadth and richness of British films on offer mean that our national cinema is on one of its many peaks – it is a cinema that celebrates, and where necessary, criticises, our country and culture. It is also means that British cinema does not just have to be Working Title, Bond movies and the Harry Potter franchise. It includes those elements certainly, and quite rightly – but there is much, much more to see, experience and enjoy that is both 'British' and 'cinema'.

# Figure 2 UK Cinema Admission 1984–2003

| | |
|---|---|
| 1984 | 54 million |
| 1985 | 72m (first UK multiplex opens) |
| 1986 | 75.5m |
| 1987 | 78.5m |
| 1988 | 84 m |
| 1989 | 94.5m |
| 1990 | 97.4m |
| 1991 | 100.3m |
| 1992 | 103.7m |
| 1993 | 114.4m |
| 1994 | 123.5m |
| 1995 | 114.6m |
| 1996 | 123.8m |
| 1997 | 139.3m |
| 1998 | 135.5m |
| 1999 | 139.8m |
| 2000 | 142.5m |
| 2001 | 155.9m |
| 2002 | 175.9m |
| 2003 | 167.3m |

Source: Film Distributors Association

Looking at the UK cinema admissions for the last 20 years, there is certainly a correlation between the opening of the new multiplexes in 1985 and a massive return of people back to the cinema. There was a steady rise of admissions until 1994, then there was a step backwards from 123 million to 114 million in 1995 and another drop in 1998 from 139 million to 135 million. 2003 saw a drop from 175 million to 167 million, for which the unusually hot and long summer could be claimed as a factor. Down already over 2 million in the first three months of 2004 compared to 2003, could it be that the mainstream multiplex blockbuster saturation releases have at last satiated the public? Now *The Lord of the Rings* trilogy has been completed, maybe there is nowhere else to go but to smaller and better productions.

# Institutions and Organisations

## 1. THE UK FILM COUNCIL

### What is it?

The UK Film Council (UKFC) is the lead agency for film in the UK, covering the economic, cultural and educational areas, and representing the UK cinema industry abroad.

Established by the Labour government in 2000, the Film Council (now re-branded as the UK Film Council) has mainly been concerned with the economics of film production, attempting to create a healthy, competitive UK film production base. It has assisted with the funding of a range of titles including *Gosford Park* (2001), *Bend It Like Beckham*, *24 Hour Party People* and *Anita and Me*.

### What does it do?

As well as supporting film production, the UKFC also has a remit to invest in a series of other initiatives including:

### The Regional Screen Agencies

Nine organisations across England set up to administer UKFC funding (around £7.5 million in 2003) to film projects, cinemas and film clubs, production companies, and training initiatives. Examples are Northern Film and Media based in Newcastle Upon Tyne, North West Vision based in Manchester and South West Screen, based in Bristol.

### Distribution and Exhibition

There are two major initiatives here that will allow more

people the chance to see a wider range of films (though not neccessarily all from the UK).

**The Digital Screen Network Fund** will allow theatrical and non-theatrical (that is, non-cinema based) venues to project films on DVD or video which will provide greater accessibility for non-mainstream work (i.e. silent cinema, classics, foreign language films) for groups like film societies, schools and community groups. It will also allow new film-makers to show their work without having to pay for a massively expensive transfer to 16mm or 35mm film prints.

Eventually it is hoped that films will be screened via computers or the web and transmitted 'down the line' without any traditional projection equipment.

The other major initiative with regard to film distribution is the **Distribution and Exhibition Publicity and Advertising Fund**, which can pay for increased publicity and advertising space and also increase the number of prints available to screen.

Nine films were supported between June and December 2003 including *Belleville Rendezvous* (2003), *Whale Rider* (2003) and *Goodbye Lenin!* (2003). These films already had a certain amount of cross-over appeal – that is to say they may have played successfully in a small amount of art-house screens – but could also appeal to a more mainstream audience, if only those audiences had more chances to see them.

The most successful proved to be the New Zealand family drama *Whale Rider*, which brought in around £1.4million at the UK box office and was nominated for a number of international awards.

Although only one of the nine films was British (*Young Adam* (2003)) the scheme was arguably a great success, as it brought a range of World Cinema titles to British audiences who may otherwise never have experienced them.

## The British Film Institute
See pg. 51 for details.

## Publishing
The UKFC supports a range of specialised cinema publications such as *Vertigo* and *Black Film-maker Magazine* which are non-profit making and which continue to provide debate and discussion about current issues in film.

## Film Production
The money UKFC invests comes from both the government, via the Department of Media Culture and Sport (DCMS), and cash raised from the National Lottery and it is likely that any UK produced film or major UK co-production released over the last 3 years would have had some input from the Film Council at some time.

Films are funded via a series of different channels:

- *The Premiere Fund*, which looks at financing commercial mainstream titles with a broad international appeal. Recent examples have included *Mike Basset, England Manager* (2001); *Gosford Park; Sylvia* (2003).

- *The New Cinema Fund*, which helps to support more specialised, independent work and 'cutting edge film-making' particularly assisting with productions from the English regions. Recent examples have included *Bloody Sunday; The Magdalene Sisters* (2002).

- *The Development Fund*, which can assist film-makers to get ideas off the ground, concentrating specifically on raising the quality of screenwriters. Recent examples have included *Kiss of Life* (2003); *Trauma* (2003).

Funding feature films is a complex combination of private and public money, overseas investment, bidding

*Funding feature films is a complex*
*Combination of private/public money, overseas*
*Investments +*

wars between sales agents and distributors, and sponsorship deals. What the UK Film Council has done for budding movie-makers is to at least give them one place to go first in search of funding, advice and support.

Although there has been a number of successful initiatives funded by the UKFC, as well as a stream of critically and commercially successful films, there has also been some criticism of it as an organisation, mainly from areas of the right wing tabloid press attacking the fact the 'public money' has been used to fund a 'vile sex film' such as *Sex Lives of The Potato Men* (2004).[15]

Criticism is not just levelled at the content of some UKFC funded films, but the fact that they are not 'value for money', losing money at the box office and unable to compete in the international market. However, using the films in the table on pg. 50 as examples, there are some points to be made clear on the costs and box office returns of films:

1. The UKFC does not fund *all* aspects of a film. Their input maybe only a small part of the income raised by a production company and funders, of which there may be many. They could be made up from TV companies such as BBC, private finance firm sponsors or individuals, sometimes even the cast and crew themselves. It's also not unheard of that members of the public send in money in return for a credit on screen and a share in the films profits.

2. UK box office income is only part of the income that that title could generate in its lifetime. There will be box office returns from different world territories when it's released in the USA, Europe, Asia and Australasia. There will also be income from television rights, satellite broadcasting, DVD and video sales and any merchandise. This does not all come back to the UKFC of course, but the added income allows the film to pay back its loan if that is what has been agreed.

3. Box office income does not all go back to the film-makers. After VAT is deducted, a percentage is given to the film distributor which could be between 35–60 per cent and the cinema exhibiting the film is left with the rest. So, if a film makes £1million at the box office, the rough sums would look like this:

**£1,000,000 in gross UK box office takings**
**minus VAT @ 17.5 per cent = £175,000**
**which leaves £825,000**

*minus* **distributor share of 45 per cent = £371,250**
**which leaves £435,750**

*minus* **UKFC investment payback of = £200,000**
**which leaves £235,750**

*minus* **payback for other investors = £121,500**
**which leaves £114,250**

There might also be other payments such as bank loans, outstanding bills and payments, or percentage cuts for some cast and crew who have deferred on a salary and opted for profit share in the profits.

Unless a British film has the backing in terms of money, resources, expertise and sheer clout from a major US studio (Working Title films has Universal, Harry Potter has Warner Bros., the Bond movies have MGM, United Artists and 20th Century Fox) it will be very hard for it to make a profit.

# Figure 3
## Examples of feature films partly funded by UKFC 2000-2004

| Selection of titles | UK box office<br>@18 April 2004 |
| --- | --- |
| ANITA AND ME (total UKFC funding, £703, 175) | £1.85 million |
| BEND IT LIKE BECKHAM (£945,043) | £11.5 million |
| BLOODY SUNDAY (£299,500) | £5000 |
| CRUSH (£875,000) | £170,000 |
| GOSFORD PARK (£2,000,000) | £12.26 million |
| THE IMPORTANCE OF BEING EARNEST (£1,320,000) | £3.52 million |
| LAWLESS HEART (£200,000) | £321,000 |
| MIKE BASSETT: ENGLAND MANAGER (£2,103,000) | £3.56 million |
| MORVERN CALLAR (£500,000) | £387,000 |
| ONCE UPON A TIME IN THE MIDLANDS (£750,000) | £494,000 |
| REVENGERS TRAGEDY (£510,000) | £42,000 |
| SEX LIVES OF THE POTATO MEN (£1,105,588) | £826,000 |
| SYLVIA (£37,643) | £444,000 |
| TOUCHING THE VOID (£392,351) | £2.41 million |

Source: *Producing the Goods? UK Film production since 1991* (BFI Information Services) and statistics from UK Film Council website

# 2. THE BRITISH FILM INSTITUTE

## What is it?

A non profit making cultural organisation, the British Film Institute (BFI) was set up in 1933 to 'encourage the art of the film'. It is now the country's main centre for film culture and education. Based (surprise, surprise) in London, at the time of writing it is in the process of a re-organisation, re-structure and public consultation, one of many over the last 10 years.

It is now funded by the UK Film Council (£16 million annually from 2004) and also generates its own income (approximately £13 million annually) through various activities and services including film distribution and publishing.

## What does it do?

In its own words the BFI:

- ensures UK audiences gain access to the full range of the history and heritage of British and international cinema;

- creates opportunities for UK citizens to understand and appreciate film through the generation and dissemination of knowledge about film;

- Promotes the use of film history in understanding identity, representation, culture and creativity.

It is responsible for a range of initiatives including:

### The National Film Theatre (NFT)

Based on the South Bank of the Thames, this is a three screen cinema complex where a range of classic and contemporary films are shown, complemented by introductions and talks by a series of film and media professionals.

Source: above information taken from the memo submitted to the House of Commons Select Committee on Culture Media and Sport, 2003.

## National Film and Television Archive (NFTVA)

A huge archive of film and television material from the 1890s to the present day, in an underground complex in Berkhamsted, Hertfordshire. The BFI is constantly in the process of restoring damaged prints and transferring dangerous material (i.e. inflammable) on to digital format. A truly unique resource that the BFI are also attempting to make more accessible to the public.

## Film Festivals

Including the London Film Festival and the Lesbian and Gay Film Festival (selections from both also tour the UK).

## Distribution

The BFI did have a production arm, giving film-makers such as Terence Davies, Derek Jarman and Peter Greenaway their first releases in the UK. Now its film distribution is mainly concentrated on new print re-issues of classic World Cinema, with recent titles including *All Quiet on the Western Front* (1930), Chaplin's *The Great Dictator* (1940) and F.W. Murnau's *Sunrise* (1927).

## Publishing

*Sight and Sound,* the monthly film magazine, is produced by the BFI and there is also a wide range of books and journals produced including the BFI Classics series, film/media text books as well as videos and DVD's of classic and contemporary World Cinema.

The key element in the BFI's work is education – that is, work with formal education (i.e. schools, colleges, universities, academics) and informal education (life-long learning, out-of school projects, adult education). There are a number of initiatives and projects currently running with direct relevance to British cinema, including Media Studies Conferences for teachers and education workers (one at the South Bank Centre in the summer and one in Bradford in the autumn) and a wealth of study guides, downloadable material, research information and web links.

# 3. PRODUCTION, DISTRIBUTION AND EXHIBITION

Since the invention of cinema at the end of the 19th century, there have always been three main areas concerned with getting films on screen and in front of audiences: **production**, **distribution** and **exhibition**.

Production was, is and probably always will be, the most written about and the most discussed of the three. It is how films are created. It concerns stars, special effects, billion dollar budgets, walkabouts at premieres and Oscars. It's the glamour and the glitz. It's Hollywood.

However, without the other two equally important links in the chain, we would never see the films that are created.

'Distribution' and 'exhibition' are virtually unknown worlds to the general cinema-goer – they may have heard the terms but know very little detail about what constitutes a distributor or the difference between an art house cinema and a multiplex.

## Production

The UK does not have the massive studio structure that Hollywood has in terms of producing films but there are now many more ways in which a film can be produced in the UK than ever before and it is almost impossible to find out about in detail, because of the myriad of companies and consortia involved and the legal and financial minefield about rights, loans, investment deals, tax breaks and funding criteria involved.

In the past, there were great British studios that produced successful films, some of which became international hits, for example, Denham Studios, Ealing Studios and the Hammer Studios in Bray. However, during the 1970s and 1980s, film-making in the UK became more and more reliant on Hollywood funding and therefore, cultural and artistic influence.

In May 1997, at the Cannes Film Festival, the Labour government announced that £92.25 million pounds of lottery funding was to be designated from the Department of Culture Media and Sport over six years to create three UK mini-studios to produce successful British films that could compete in the international market place and make a profit for funders and investors.

Bids had been invited from interested consortia and the three successful 'studios' were:

- **PATHÉ PRODUCTIONS** – created from the old Guild Distribution Company and whose other partners included Rupert Murdoch's BSkyB, Studio CanalPlus from France and Mike Leigh's production company, Thin Man Films.

- **THE FILM CONSORTIUM** – partners included Scala Productions and Virgin, whose previous hits had included *The Crying Game* (1992) and *Michael Collins* (1996).

- **DNA FILMS** – headed by Duncan Kenworthy (producer of *Notting Hill* and *Four Weddings...*) and Andrew MacDonald (producer of *Trainspotting* and *Shallow Grave*, among others).

The funding given by the DCMS was not to fund all costs for production – each company would have to find the rest of the finance themselves either through co-production deals with other countries (usually Europe or the US), loans, grants from other organisations or private investment. The companies gained some successes: Pathé for example produced *Chicken Run* (1999) and *Girl with a Pearl Earring* (2003) and has recently seen mountaineering drama documentary *Touching the Void* (2003) take over £2.4 million at the UK box office.

DNA Films and The Film Consortium have had varying degrees of success. DNA has only released six titles to date including Danny Boyle's horror zombie sleeper hit, *28 Days Later* and were also one of the many hands in *Love Actually*. A comedy starring Ian Hart, *Strictly Sinatra* (2001) and Steve Coogan's comedy *The Parole Officer* (2001) proved less successful. They are now 50 per cent owned by Fox Searchlight, the 'indie' arm of 20th Century Fox.

The Film Consortium has not been as successful at the UK box office as was hoped, with *Fanny and Elvis* (1998) only taking £162,000 and *Janice Beard: 45 wpm* (1999) bringing in around £9000. Although titles such as *Hideous Kinky* (1997) and Michael Winterbottom's internationally acclaimed *In This World* (2002) fared rather better (at least critically), the Lottery franchise project didn't really set up a permanent studio system creating a series of commercially successful titles for an international market place. Maybe that is impossible to do in the UK with such a diverse range of film-makers, social and ethnic groups, with many stories and ideas relevant only to a regional or even local environment.

Other ways films are funded in the UK, apart from via the three above companies are:

- Part funding from the UK Film Council (see section on UKFC).

- In partnership with a US studio (i.e. Working Title and

Universal) who will add funding and distribute the film across the US and Europe.

- Assistance with funding from one of the Regional Screen Agencies across the UK who may help with finding crews, training, seed/development funding for scripts, funding of a short film that can be used as a 'calling card' for a director.

- Investment from Europe – *Bend It Like Beckham* had assistance from the Hamburg Film Fund in return for shooting some sequences in Germany, Mike Leigh has a deal with CanalPlus in France for part-funding of his films and Ken Loach's *Sweet Sixteen* had investment from Germany (Wim Wenders's Road Movie company) and Spain.

- The Isle of Man Film Commission – a surprisingly lucrative deal in which the Commission invests in a film in return for the production shooting there and using Manx personnel. Thus a film such as *I Capture the Castle* (2003) gets lovely scenery and there is work for the islanders (and presumably some tax/VAT deal which is beneficial to all concerned but is too complicated to go into here).

- BBC TV is still an important source of British cinema by funding (or part funding) work for the small screen but which is then released into cinemas (i.e. *Persuasion* and *Mrs Brown*).

# Distribution

## What is a distributor?

A distributor is the link between the film-makers and the public, and allows a film to reach the public via the cinemas, DVD/video and on television. There are a number of distribution companies in the UK, all with different styles, funding structures, aims and marketing plans, all trying to sell their films in an incredibly competitive environment.

Each distribution company takes on a certain number of titles each year and creates an individual release-plan for those films. There responsibilities include:

- deciding on a release date;
- deciding how many prints to produce and in which cinemas to screen them;
- advertising campaigns;
- designing art work for adverts, posters, flyers and bill-boards;
- organising premieres and talker screenings;
- booking talent (i.e. the stars or director) for press interviews and personal appearances.

Distributors are also responsible for negotiating deals regarding the film's release on video and DVD, and showings on television, cable and satellite channels.

A film could come to the distributor in a range of ways – films produced by the main American studios will be distributed through their own companies, so Warner Bros. will distribute their own films as will 20<sup>th</sup> Century Fox and Buena Vista International will distribute Disney films as it is the Disney distribution 'arm'.

Some films are seen at film festivals and are picked up through complicated negotiations with sales agents and producers so deals can be struck in different territories (i.e. North America, Europe, Asia, Australasia).

## Types of UK distributors
In the UK, distributors are divided into the **majors** and the **independents**.

## The majors
The majors are those affiliated to the biggest Hollywood companies and are:

Warner Bros, Fox, Columbia Tri Star.
UIP Buena Vista (All us)

Warner Bros.;
20th Century Fox;
Columbia Tri-Star;
Buena Vista International (BVI, owned by the Disney Corporation);
United International Pictures (UIP, who release films from Universal and MGM studios).

The films released by the majors tend to be mainstream Hollywood blockbusters as well as UK/USA co-productions such as *Bridget Jones's Diary, Love Actually* and *Calendar Girls*. Some companies have an 'indie' arm such as Fox Searchlight or Focus Features (Universal) that will take risks on films that are not such commercial blockbusters.

## The Independents

These are companies who release a much wider range of films, and include Artificial Eye, Pathé, Metro Tartan, Metrodome, Momentum and Contemporary. Titles will include foreign language films, documentaries, re-releases and non-mainstream Hollywood/UK titles picked up at film festivals across the world.

Entertainment Distribution is an unusual case in that it is a UK independent that has a long standing relationship with US studio New Line Cinema (a unit of the Time Warner corporation). Entertainment release their titles in the UK, therefore getting such films as *Lord Of the Rings* as well as small UK titles such as *Sex Lives of the Potato Men* and *Charlie* (2004). (The vast majority of Entertainment's 14.5 per cent market share in the table opposite will have come from the second and third films in *The Lord of the Rings* trilogy, both on release in 2003).

Organisations such as the BFI and the Institute of Contemporary Art (ICA) as well as some Regional Film Theatres (RFTs) also pick up the rights of films for a limited distribution and also co-ordinate touring packages where it's possible to see new titles without a distribution deal, although usually for only on or two screenings per title in each venue.

Recent tours have included retrospectives of Bergman and Visconti from the BFI, and Festivals such as the London Lesbian and Gay Film Festival, the Sheffield Documentary Film Festival, the Manchester Cornerhouse VIVA Spanish Cinema Festival and the London Film Festival on Tour.

*Looking at the information in Figure 4 below from the Film Distributor Association, it is obvious (perhaps frighteningly so) how much of what we see is determined by American studios and distributors. In terms of British distribution companies, only Pathé, Entertainment and Momentum are mentioned, and between them the 5 majors account for over 78 per cent market share for films released in the UK in 2003.*

## Figure 4 UK film distributor market share 2003

| UK film distributor | No. new releases 2003 | %Market share 2003 |
|---|---|---|
| Buena Vista International (UK) | 37 | 26.6% |
| UIP | 28 | 22.5% |
| Entertainment Film Distributors | 17 | 14.5% |
| Warner Bros. | 17 | 10.4% |
| Columbia Tri-Star Films UK | 31 | 9.8% |
| 20th Century Fox | 25 | 8.8% |
| Pathé | 22 | 1.9% |
| Momentum Pictures | 20 | 1.4% |
| Icon Film Distribution | 8 | 0.7% |
| Others (including non-FDA members) | 218 | 3.7% |
| Total | 423 | 100% |

Source: Nielsen EDI

## Acquiring a film

A distributor can acquire the rights to release a film in the UK in a number of different ways:

- directly from their parent studio (i.e. Warner Bros.; Fox; Universal through UIP);

- through a deal a distributor may have with a production company or studio;

- a distributor may be approached by a third party sales agent;

- a distributor may attend a film festival and approach a sales agent after watching a film at a screening.

A distribution deal is different for every film, and will include theatrical rights (i.e. the screening of the film in cinemas), and possibly the release of the film on DVD and video as well as TV and satellite rights.

# Releasing a film

Many things have to be taken into consideration when distributors choose a release date for a movie. School holidays in Easter, half term, summer and Christmas tend to be the time when big family movies are set for release. Big football events, particularly when England are taking part, such as the European Championships and the World Cup can affect audiences, so care is taken about releasing male-orientated, action-type movies at that time.

It is also crucial to know the landscape with regard to film and media related events happening nationally and most importantly, what else is being released at the time. The last thing you want is your film being released on the same weekend as *The Lord of the Rings: The Return of the King* (2003) or *Star Wars Episode III* (2005), both of which will swamp the media and the national consciousness (unless, that is, you are consciously positioning the marketing strategy in opposition to these blockbusters).

## Release patterns

There are basically three types of release in the UK:

### Saturation –

a film that literally saturates the country in terms of number of prints and national publicity, i.e. *The Lord Of The Rings*, the Harry Potter series, *The Matrix* sequels (2003). These are usually films backed by the major Hollywood studios and will have had an extremely large publicity and production budget behind them. There will also be advertising tie-ins to high street companies and merchandising spin-offs such as computer games, books, magazines and a TV *Making of…* documentary.

The films will also have almost as much publicity when they are released, only a few months later, on DVD and video.

In terms of screenings, films like *The Lord Of The Rings* will be shown up to 12–15 times a day at most multiplexes even three or four weeks after their release.

Posters will be on key billboard and bus shelters sites, and recognisable images will usually feature on magazine covers with saturation coverage inside. In *Empire* for example, each month the cover and dozens of inside pages are given over to one new blockbuster film in terms of articles, reviews, interviews and adverts. In *Empire*'s July 1999 issue, over 50 per cent of the pages in the magazine featured articles, adverts and interviews about *Star Wars Episode I: The Phantom Menace* (1999), and 34 pages in the June 2003 issue are dedicated to the *The Matrix Reloaded*. The July 2003 issue saw *The Hulk* (2003) dominating and the final film in *The Lord of the Rings* trilogy had blanket coverage in the January 2004 issue.

This massive coverage is something that seems to be unstoppable and is worth considering when American film industry executives such as Motion Picture Association of America (MPAA) head honcho Jack Valenti talk about 'healthy competition' in Europe. There is no serious competition – Hollywood majors, unsurprisingly, sweep all aside.

The number of prints for a saturation release can range from 600–800 and will screen at all the major cinema chains (i.e. Odeon, UCI, UGC, Warners), as well as high street commercial independents such as City Screen sites, opening across the country on the same day. It is now usual for the biggest films to have 1 or 2 days of 'preview screenings' before the Friday opening.

## Wide release –

still a large release, but not on the same scale as the blockbusters mentioned above. There will usually be around 100 prints. These titles are also known as 'cross-over' films, as they may also screen at subsidised independent cinemas as well as multiplexes. The film may open in London, gradually spreading across the country over the next few weeks.

Recent example of wide release title – *Girl with a Pearl Earring.*

## Limited release –

a small scale release, around 10–20 prints. Titles are usually known as 'art house' or 'specialised' films and will play in the Regional Film Theatres (RFT's), the National Film Theatre in London and some City Screen sites. Films will tend to be foreign language titles, re-released classics, small independent English language titles. Some films may have as little as 4 or 5 prints, and if it's a film touring as part of a festival (i.e. The London Film Festival on Tour), only 1 print may be available.

Recent example of limited release title – *In This World.*

# Costs

Cinemas will pay distributors a percentage of net box office, which is usually between 35–60 per cent but may be higher for some multiplex chains for franchises such as James Bond, Harry Potter, *The Lord of the Rings*, etc. In the case of smaller cinemas that may get the film on a second run or may screen a classic repertory title, the rental fee may be around 25–30 per cent or may be a minimum guarantee of around £80–100.

# Exhibition

This is the process of showing a film to an audience, mainly referring to a cinema environment, but with the advent of new digital projection equipment and DVD players, screenings in schools, colleges, art centres and outdoor venues are future possibilities.

In the UK, there are three main types of cinema exhibition environments:

## Multiplex/Megaplex
A North American concept, the first UK cinema opening in Milton Keynes in 1985 owned by the American Multi-Cinema Corporation (AMC). There are now a number of chains such as UGC, UCI, Warner Village and MGM. Most Odeon cinemas outside London also now have multiplex sites, although some are still 4–5 screen high street sites.

Most are multi-national corporations with many, many tentacles of ownership:

- **Warners** is now **Vue**, a company owned by SBC Cinemas, owned by a group of US financial and legal firms;

- **UCI** is owned by Universal and Paramount Pictures;

- **Odeon** is now co-owned by German Bank WestLB, The Entertainment Group and an individual called Robert Tchenguiz (who he is I'm not exactly sure);

- **UGC** is owned by UGC France who also have a distribution arm.

The number of screens can range from 12–15, and in some cases up to 25, such as Star City in Birmingham. However, this 'megaplex', which boasted shops, restaurants, a tattoo bar and screens that were to be dedicated to art house and Bollywood fare, has proved to be problematic. While there is a greater representation

# Figure 5 British cinema at the UK box office

An example of box office data for the weekend of 16th–18th April 2004 is shown opposite.

The only UK film in the top 15 is horror spoof *Shaun of the Dead*, which has made a healthy £4.35 million (column 9) in 2 weeks (column 7), although it has been co-funded and distributed by a US company.

The '% change column' refers to the negative downturn or positive improvement of box office take week on week – i.e. *Shaun of the Dead*'s box office this weekend is 29 per cent down on last weekend. Usually, films gradually take less and less as the weeks go on, so the figure is always usually negative. Where there is no figure, it is the film's first week on release.

In column 8, 'number of cinemas' refers to the number of cinema sites the film has been sent to – there actually may be more than one copy of the film at that site. In the case of *The Lord of the Rings* or Harry Potter films, it could be playing at 4 or 5 screens on the same day.

As of this weekend in April 2004, the running total box office from the top 15 films showing in the UK was £65,098,567. Out of that, £58,225,961 was taken by US companies – 89.4 per cent. This is a fairly typical ratio, and £8,696,134 a fairly typical weekend's takings.

© UIP

**SHUFFLING TO SUCCESS: SHAUN OF THE DEAD IS ONE OF THE MOST CRITICALLY AND COMMERCIALLY SUCCESSFUL BRITISH COMEDIES OF RECENT YEARS**

| 1 | 2 | 3 | 4 | 5 | 6 | 7 | 8 | 9 |
|---|---|---|---|---|---|---|---|---|
| Rank | Title | Country of Origin | Gross | Distributor | % change on last week | Weeks on release | Number of cinemas | Total to date |
| 1 | Scooby-Doo Too | USA | £1,772,130 | Warner | -13 | 3 | 487 | £13,145,710 |
| 2 | 50 First Dates | USA | £1,196,553 | Col/Tri-Star | -28 | 2 | 395 | £4,356,363 |
| 3 | Shaun of the Dead | UK | £1,132,177 | UIP | -29 | 2 | 369 | £4,111,134 |
| 4 | The Cat in the Hat | USA | £780,754 | UIP | -12 | 3 | 441 | £6,313,021 |
| 5 | The Butterfly Effect | USA | £735,287 | Icon | - | 1 | 276 | £735,287 |
| 6 | The Girl Next Door | USA | £713,107 | 20th Fox | - | 1 | 325 | £713,107 |
| 7 | The Passion of the Christ | USA | £564,982 | Icon | -56 | 6 | 366 | £9,479,240 |
| 8 | Gothika | USA | £495,829 | Col/Tri-Star | -41 | 3 | 308 | £4,491,633 |
| 9 | Hidalgo | USA | £446,550 | BVI | - | 1 | 293 | £446,550 |
| 10 | Starsky and Hutch | USA | £281,095 | BVI | -54 | 6 | 258 | £12,284,956 |
| 11 | Monster | USA/GER | £223,093 | Metrodome | -17 | 3 | 72 | £1,248,327 |
| 12 | Dawn of the Dead | USA | £150,647 | Entertainment | -64 | 4 | 210 | £5,434,023 |
| 13 | Barbershop 2 | USA | £73,174 | 20th Fox | - | 1 | 45 | £73,174 |
| 14 | Welcome to the Jungle | USA | £71,996 | Col/Tri-Star | -54 | 4 | 171 | £2,075,686 |
| 15 | Capturing the Friedmans | USA | £58,760 | Tartan | -17 | 2 | 26 | £190,356 |
| | Total | | £8,696,134 | | | | 4,042 | £65,098,567 |

of Asian cinema than usual for a multiplex, reflecting the local demographic, the commitment to art house cinema appears to have fallen victim to the Hollywood juggernaught.

Multiplexes claim to offer a wide range of choice, but in reality, across the country they will all play the same 8–10 core titles.

## The subsidised sector

A number of venues across the country, both full-time and part time, are revenue funded by grant-in-aid from various sources. These include the Cornerhouse in Manchester, Broadway in Nottingham, Tyneside Cinema in Newcastle and the Metro Cinema in Derby.

Simply put, the Department of Media Culture and Sport give funding to the UK Film Council, the UK Film Council give money to the Regional Screen Agencies across the country, who then give money to their revenue clients.

Each venue and organisation has to hit certain criteria before funding is given (business plans, strategies for education, marketing and artistic programming, financial forecasts, etc. are required). The venues may also get funding from local authorities, the National Lottery, sponsorship, Europe and also, of course, from the box office.

Education work and other contexualised events are integral to the work of these venues and all of them work with a wide range of groups including schools, colleges, community groups and artists.

Their programmers endeavour to put on the widest range of cinema possible, combining film screenings with a range of special events such as regional film-making forums, director/actor workshops, digital video work and mixed media events. Some venues instigate their own festivals and touring programmes including *Bite the Mango* at Bradford Pictureville, *Showcommotion* at Sheffield Showroom, *Brief Encounters Short Film Festival* at Bristol Watershed and the *Northern Lights Festival* at Tyneside Cinema in Newcastle.

## Commercial art house

A number of commercial cinemas across the country now mix art house and multiplex programming, the most successful being the City Screen chain. City Screen run the Curzon Soho Cinema in London and also a number of sites across the country in towns such as York, Stratford Upon Avon, Cambridge and Brighton where there is no other art house provision. Technical facilities are usually excellent, and most sites have a bar and restaurant.

As with multiplexes, the financing of the City Screen circuit is complicated. Their majority stakeholder is the Arts Alliance Group, which in turn is a division of the Heogh Capital Partners Advisors Ltd, based in New York and London.[16]

City Screen have also moved into the subsidised exhibition sector as they now programme the first run material for Cinema City in Norwich and Tyneside Cinema in Newcastle upon Tyne.

# And the future…

At the moment, both distribution and exhibition sectors are going though a time of massive change. The Government set up the Film Council in 2000 (now the UK Film Council, see above) to create a 'sustainable UK film industry' and there has been many changes in the funding system with various lottery schemes, new Regional Screen agencies being created, the Regional Arts Boards developing into Arts Council of England, North East/North West/South West (delete where appropriate) and staff cuts at the British Film Institute in the very areas that champion cultural exhibition. More *[handwritten: future - UKFC (set up by Gov't) to create a sustainable film industry. Lottery money also used. More]*

positively, as discussed earlier the UKFCs Specialised Prints and Advertising Fund gave £1 million in 2003 to selected distributors who wanted to create more prints and more marketing for selected non-mainstream, specialised films, which in turn will hopefully increase audience access. Titles including the Oscar nominated New Zealand drama *Whale Rider* and the German comedy *Goodbye Lenin!* reached wider audiences in more cinemas and garnering respectable box office figures as a result.[17]

It is a turbulent time, but one in which people who are passionate about cinema in all its forms (in the education sector as well as the film industry) should find exciting and challenging. The films are out there somewhere, it's up to us to find them.

## SOME KEY UK FILM DISTRUBUTORS

### ARTIFICIAL EYE
A champion of bringing challenging World Cinema into the UK and in front of audiences in cinemas. Recent titles have included *Russian Ark* (2002) and Takeshi Kitano's *Zatoichi* (2003).
**www.artificial-eye.com**

### MOMENTUM
Site under construction but information on new releases available via email.
**www.momentumpictures.co.uk**

### ICA
The Institute of Contemporary Art in the Mall in London has a film distribution arm, and an eclectic and astonishingly varied back catalogue of titles.
Recent releases include Michael Winterbottom's *In This World*.
**www.ica.org.uk**

## METRO TARTAN

Website not updated since May 2002, but an energetic distributor of films often on the fringes of the mainstream, such as *Audition* (2000), *Être et avoir* (2003) and *Capturing the Friedmans* (2003).
**www.metro-tartan.co.uk**

## CONTEMPORARY

A great back catalogue of World Cinema classics, with an unashamedly politically liberal slant.
**www.contemporaryfilms.com**

## PATHÉ

A mixture of art house and mainstream (recent titles have included *Buffalo Soldiers*, *Touching the Void* and *Girl with a Pearl Earring*).
**www.pathe.co.uk (website under construction at time of writing)**

## METRODOME

Responsible for bringing some excellent popular World Cinema into the UK including Lukas Moodysson's *Together* (2000), *The Experiment* (2001) and *Divided We Fall* (2000).
**www.metrodomegroup.com**

## ENTERTAINMENT

A UK independent but one that has an agreement to release films from the US through the New Line Studio, so their titles include massive worldwide blockbusters such as *The Lord of the Rings* trilogy as well as smaller British films such as *Sex Lives Of the Potato Men*.
**www.lordoftherings.net**

*An earlier version of the DISTRIBUTION and EXHIBITION section was published in IN THE PICTURE No. 47, September 2003.*

# Genre and Representation in Recent British Cinema: Films in Close-Up

In this section, I want to examine five recent British films in five different genres in some detail, looking at the background to the production, cast and creative crew, how the film represents 'Britishness' and the British, and how it relates to its historical and cultural context as well as the potential audience it was aimed at.

There are also suggestions for further viewing of related films you may find useful and enjoyable to use as tools when teaching students.

## The Youth Film: Film as Fashion Accessory

**TRAINSPOTTING (1996)**
Director: Danny Boyle
Screenplay: John Hodge, based on the novel by Irvine Welsh
Songs include: *Lust for Life* and *Nightclubbing* (Iggy Pop);

*Temptation* (Heaven 17); *Atomic* and *Statuesque* (Sleeper); *Sing* (Blur); *Perfect Day* (Lou Reed); *Mile End* (Pulp); *2.1* (Elastica); *Born Slippy* (Underworld)

**Renton** ....................................Ewan McGregor
**Spud** ........................................Ewen Bremner
**Sick Boy** ..................................Jonny Lee Miller
**Tommy** ....................................Kevin McKidd
**Begbie** .....................................Robert Carlyle
**Diane**........................................Kelly Macdonald
**Swanney** ..................................Peter Mullan
**Mr Renton** ..............................James Cosmo
**Gail**...........................................Shirley Henderson
**Mikey** ......................................Irvine Welsh
**Drug Dealer** ...........................Keith Allen
**Andreas** ...................................Kevin Allen
**Game Show host**...................Dale Winton

**Released in the UK: February 1996**
**Budget £1.76 million**
**UK Box office £12.4 million**

*Available on Universal DVD and VHS.*
*DVD includes audio commentary including Danny Boyle and Ewan McGregor, deleted scenes, documentaries on the look of the film and the music, trailers and photo galleries.*

## The film in context

Looking back to the heady days of early 1996, when every new film with a pop soundtrack and in a club scene was hailed as the great new British youth movie, it is difficult to understand the impact *Trainspotting* had, not only on the film industry, but in design, music, fashion and drug culture. The soundtrack became an anthem for the summer of '96, the publicity poster and adverts were vibrant and imaginative, with the cast standing in a line, bold nametags announcing their arrival in a flash of day glow orange. The shaven head and blanched pasty skin of Renton became *de rigueur* for thousands of lads across the country on their nights out.

"Trainspotting is the best British film of the decade" ★★★★★ EMPIRE

**18**

Trainspotting

DVD

UNIVERSAL

**THE TRAINSPOTTING CREW IN FULL ON FASHION MODE**

Lou Reed and Iggy Pop were rediscovered by a new generation (particularly ironic was the use of Reed's soporific *Perfect Day* [as used in the film when Renton heads off on a 'trip'] as a mass sing-along by BBC Children in Need) and Ewan McGregor was set on the road to superstardom, with Robert Carlyle not far behind.

*Trainspotting* was unique at the time for a number of reasons. It took on a difficult subject as its key element (drugs, particularly heroin, had been the then Conservative government's *bête noir*, with a massively expensive 'shock horror' poster and TV ad campaign which didn't really tackle the roots of the problem). It also gave the world a unique view of a much loved British city, Edinburgh, without showing the tourist trail sights (castle, Hollyrood Palace, Royal Mile, Princes' Street), but portraying it as a world of tenements, back streets and dark, unfurnished drug dens full of squatters. It was the world of Robert Louis Stephenson, an Edinburgh writer whose masterwork, *The Strange Tale of Dr Jekyll and Mr Hyde* was influenced by the two faces of the city he lived in – the clean, ordered New Town, and the dark, dangerous underworld Old Town on castle hill.

One other aspect of the press coverage given to the film was the amazingly wide range of copy headlines in paper and magazines to introduce articles, including 'No Anoraks Allowed' (Film Review, March 1996), 'First Class Return' (Empire, February 1996) and perhaps the best of all, 'Hey Hey it's the Junkies' (The Face, March 1996).

The film was born from the collaboration of director Danny Boyle, writer John Hodge and producer Andrew Macdonald, who had worked together (with McGregor) on *Shallow Grave*, a savagely funny black comedy about money and greed among a trio of flat-mates set in Glasgow. Hodge read Irvine Welsh's scabrous tale of psychos, no-hopers and addicts – the characters are not only addicted to drugs, but to their lifestyle – and pitched it to his colleagues as their next project.

They approached Channel Four (who had backed *Shallow Grave*) with a draft script, the project was given the green light and shooting began in May 1995, mainly around Glasgow. Only two days of exterior shots were filmed in Edinburgh itself.

Released on the same day in February 1996 as *Sense And Sensibility* (two British films as far away from each other as you could get), *Trainspotting* was an immediate hit at the box office, though not with all the critics. The popular glossy monthlies gave it a definite thumbs up (*Film Review* and *Empire* both gave it 5 stars), and Derek Malcolm in *The Guardian* described it as '*an extraordinary achievement and a breakthrough British film*' (February 22, 1996).

However, *The Times* was scathing, described it as '*utterly empty...a cold turkey, despite the fancy trimmings*' (February 22, 1996) and, more interestingly, accused the film of '*spend(ing) far too much time with its nose pressed up against the glass of American cinema, desperate for a piece of the action*'. However, the film, with its music, sets, costumes, style of acting and mix of realism and surrealism is perhaps as far away from mainstream American cinema at that time as it could possibly be.

There *are* influences of Tarantino in the violent outbursts of Begbie, perhaps, and in the fast moving camera (zooms, pans, freeze frames). But where Tarantino associates violence and death with an underlying feeling cool and hipness, there is nothing cool about Begbie's glass fight in the London pub, or the death of Tommy, or the fate of Allison's baby and its horrific aftermath for Renton.

# What does the film say? Language and Representation

The film opens with Iggy Pop's thunderous *Lust For Life* on the soundtrack as we meet each character, and over Renton's introductory rant against consumerism and suburban normality, *'Choose Life...'*.

**LUST FOR LIFE: RENTON AND SPUD ON THE STREETS OF EDINBURGH**

The film's use of music is crucial to its style, as each track is a direct comment on the action or thoughts of the characters, not only lyrically (Renton does indeed have a lust for life) but in the sound. The track thunders and pounds along just as Renton and the gang do through the backstreets of Edinburgh. *Perfect Day* does the same, as it's languid, dreamy tune relates directly with Renton's experience after his heroin hit.

The characters, particularly Spud, Renton and Sick Boy, although they are in some ways dangerous and unattractive (their living habits, their drug taking via needle) have characteristics the audience can emphathise with. As the *Trainspotting* audience would mostly be in their late teens and twenties, Renton's opening shout against normality would have certainly struck a chord with viewers, even though the majority of them *would* have CD players and televisions, and *would* watch mind numbing games shows on couches, probably studying for degrees at the same time. Through Sick Boy's 'sick' humour, such as shooting air rifle pellets up a dog's rectum in the park (while doing an excellent Sean Connery impression, it must be said), and Spud's appealing gormlessness (particularly in the job interview scene and the horrendous accident with stained sheets at Gail's house), we become involved in the characters stories, even though they may have some deeply unpleasant habits.

Another reason we can emphathise with them and why they perhaps seem so appealing, is because the character of Begbie is so extreme (perhaps because that character is frighteningly familiar to audiences across the UK, whether standing in a packed city centre bar, at a taxi queue at night or sitting opposite you in a train packed with soccer fans). Begbie's violence is sometimes very funny (the scene in which he nonchalantly tosses his beer glass over his shoulder and over a balcony never failed to get a roar of laughter each of the 11 times I saw the film when I was working at Tyneside Cinema covering usher shifts) but he is also a deeply unpleasant, damaged person who makes the rest of the gang seem harmless, damaging only themselves.

Danny Boyle's use of different shooting styles (hand held, speeded up, slow motion) give the film a feeling of non-stop motion, of speed, which combined with the soundtrack is certainly an exhilarating experience.

Two of the most controversial aspects of the film were the attitude towards drugs, heroin in particular, and the portrayal of Scotland. In the case of drugs, it certainly cannot be seen as an advert for taking heroin. While the characters can be seen as cool and funny, their lifestyle is pretty mundane and unexciting. After a hit, Renton and Sick Boy are shown almost comatose, their squat is dirty and cold, and Renton's withdrawal from the drug is horrific as he witnesses a vision of Allison' dead baby crawling towards him.

However, the film-makers did not want to gloss over the drug culture so attempted to show it 'as it was' with advice from Calton Athletic Drug Rehab Centre in Glasgow, with recovering heroin user Eamon Doherty as the film's technical advisor. The close-up scenes of injection, the pain of trying to find a useful vein and the 'coming down' after a hit are graphically shown as well as letting the audience feel the high that's achieved. As screenwriter John Hodge has explained, 'Some people would have you believe that heroin is unpleasant and it destroys your life. The fact is that it's *pleasant* and destroys your life'. (*Northern Echo*, 7 March 96).

The film also shows a very different view of Edinburgh and Scotland from that usually seen in the mainstream media. Ironically, for most media and film professionals, the only view of Edinburgh they get is when visiting the Film Festival in August, shuffling between the Film House Cinema and the Film Centre two hundred yards away, perhaps venturing to a bar or club in the Old Town at night.

Very little of the film was actually shot in Edinburgh (one key scene shot there was the shoplifting sequence and the chase along Prince's Street) but it's the attitude the film shows towards Scotland and its heritage that is refreshing, particularly in the scene when Tommy tries to introduce the gang to the great outdoors by taking them on a trip to the Highlands. Shown on countless adverts for Scottish Tourism and on TV programmes such as *Monarch of the Glen*, the landscape is here treated as alien and unhealthy by Sick Boy, Spud and Renton, who just want to get back to the squat. It leads Renton off on a tirade, not against the English, but against Scotland for

**THE GREAT OUTDOORS**

being conquered by the English:

*'It's shite being Scottish, we're the lowest of the low,'... 'We can't even find a decent culture to be colonised by!'*

This attitude towards the English and London in particular is reinforced in the sequence when Renton *et al* arrive in London to a sunny synthesiser dance track, with deliberately clichéd shots of Tower Bridge and Big Ben as well as an unfeasibly jolly Pearly couple. There is even shot of Spud, Renton, Sick Boy and Begbie walking across the zebra crossing, a typical tourism trick re-enacting the The Beatles' *Abbey Road* album cover.

The film has certainly not dated and indeed seems to have acquired cult status. The soundtrack became a best seller (as did volume two, of tracks 'inspired' by the film) as did the video on first release and the recent deluxe double disc DVD.

Inspiring a host of British youth films such as *Human Traffic* and *The Acid House*, *Trainspotting* had traces of past hits, in particular *A Hard Day's Night* in its use of four very different characters and its freewheeling camera work. Although not in the financial league of *Four Weddings and a Funeral* and *Notting Hill*, the film has certainly had more lasting influence on pop and film culture than either.

# THE YOUTH FILM: FURTHER VIEWING

### BOSTON KICKOUT (1995)
*Directed by Paul Hills*
*Written by Paul Hills, Diane Whitely and Roberto Troni*
Set in the concrete jungle of Stevenage and pre-dating *Trainspotting*, this has become overshadowed by later 'youth' films but has a gritty edge and energetic performances by (now) famous groups of British TV/film actors.

### LOVED UP (1995)
*Directed by Peter Cattaneo*
*Written by Oliver Parker*
A made for TV BBC drama, this is well worth catching if it is repeated (at the moment it's unavailable on video) as it's a snapshot of the early rave and drug culture in the UK (it was filmed in 1994 pre-*Trainspotting*) and is careful to balance the pros and cons (loved up dance music, seedy drug dealing, loss of dignity). The director went on to make *The Full Monty*.

### TWIN TOWN (1997)
*Directed by Kevin Allen*
*Written by Kevin Allen and Paul Durden*
Released with inevitable comparisons to *Trainspotting* given its subject matter (disaffected youth in non-English town principality, containing drugs and sex), *Twin Town* actually stands up on its own as a fast and funny take on Welsh clichés and working-class life. Like *Trainspotting* it mocks its own nationhood.

### HUMAN TRAFFIC (1999)
*Written and directed by Justin Kerrigan*
Set around the clubbing scene of Cardiff, this is an interesting comparison to *Trainspotting* in that drugs (in this case ecstasy) have ceased to be an issue and the main characters (who would have been the key demographic for *Trainspotting*) are younger, cleaner and it seems, wiser, knowing that heroin does bad things.

### MORVERN CALLAR (2002)
*Directed by Lynne Ramsay*
*Written by Lynne Ramsay and Liana Dognini, based on the novel by Alan Warner*
Hallucinatory tale of a young girl who finds her boyfriend's dead body and heads off to Ibiza with a girlfriend to grieve and party. Dance music and stunning visuals combine in this adaptation of a difficult novel.

# The Heritage Film: Viewing the Past

### ELIZABETH (1998)
Director: Shekhar Kapur
Screenplay: Michael Hirst
Music: David Hirschfelder (includes *Nimrod* by Edward Elgar and *Requiem* by Wolfgang Amadeus Mozart)

**Elizabeth**.................................Cate Blanchett
**Sir Francis Walsingham**........Geoffrey Rush
**Robert Dudley** ......................Joseph Fiennes
**The Duke of Norfolk** ............Christopher Eccleston
**Sir William Cecil** ..................Richard Attenborough
**Alvaro de la Quadra**.............James Frain
**Mary Tudor** ...........................Kathy Burke
**Duc d'Anjou** ..........................Vincent Cassel
**Mary of Guise** .......................Fanny Ardant
**Earl of Sussex** .......................Jamie Forman
**Earl of Arundel**......................Edward Hardwicke

**Monsieur de Foix**.................Eric Cantona
**Isabel Knollys**......................Kelly Macdonald
**The Pope** ..............................John Gielgud

**Released in the UK: October 1998**
**Budget: £13 million**
**UK box office: £5.53million**

*Available to buy on VHS and DVD (Polygram, Cert 15).*
*DVD extras – interviews with cast and crew; behind*
*the scenes footage; 'The Making Of* Elizabeth'
*featurette.*

## The film in context

Released in 1998, *Elizabeth* is the latest in a long line of
cinematic portraits of the monarch. Starting with Sarah
Bernhardt's delirious portrait *Queen Elizabeth* (1912), in
which Elizabeth dies in a swoon after hearing of the
death of Essex, there have been a number of films
featuring Elizabeth. Bette Davis starred in two of the
most famous 'older Elizabeth' films, *The Private Lives of
Elizabeth and Essex* (1939), co-starring Errol Flynn
playing the Earl of Essex as a vain and spoilt brat, and
*The Virgin Queen* (1955), where she romances Sir Walter
Raleigh (Richard Todd).

Flora Robson also played the Queen twice, in *Fire Over
England* (1936) and in *The Sea Hawk* (USA 1940), both
set against the attack of the Spanish Armada in 1588.

*Young Bess* (1953), is interesting as it portrays the Queen
(Jean Simmons) as a teenager, and explores her
relationship with an older man, Thomas Seymour
(Stewart Granger) – in reality, she was only 14 when he
tried to seduce her.

On television, Glenda Jackson's *Elizabeth R* (1971) was
the benchmark for historical biographical drama for years
afterwards and probably the role Jackson is most
remembered for. Another, more recent, portrayal should

not be forgotten; Miranda Richardson's Queenie in *Blackadder II* (1985) was a spoilt brat with a lisp, beheading people on a whim and giving her own spin on Elizabeth's famous speech:

> *'I may have the body of a weak and feeble woman, but I have the heart and stomach of a concrete elephant.'*

*Elizabeth* can also be compared to another film in circulation at the same time, *Shakespeare in Love*, released in the UK in January 1999, 3 months after *Elizabeth*. Both portray a very different Elizabethan England – *Shakespeare in Love* is the 'Merrie England' of myth; bawdy, theatrical, shot in bright colours and sunlight, with a wise and knowing Queen (the time is not specified in the film, but Christopher Marlow was killed in 1593, making Elizabeth 60 years old). The films are also linked by two actors, Joseph Fiennes (who plays Shakespeare), repeating a romantic hero role as Dudley and Geoffrey Rush.

*Elizabeth* did well at the UK box office, taking around £4.5 million, and gaining a number of awards including the Oscar for best make-up and BAFTAs for Cate Blanchett, Geoffrey Rush, cinematography and, again, make-up.

It also added to the growing number of recent books and television documentaries around Elizabeth and the Tudor Court, most notably David Starkey's *Henry VIII* (1998) and *Elizabeth: Apprenticeship* (2000).

The film proved to be Cate Blanchett's international breakthrough, winning 11 major awards for her role, including a BAFTA and a Golden Globe, and being nominated for an Oscar. She is now a major 'name', subsequently starring in *The Talented Mr Ripley* (1999), *The Gift* (2000), *Veronica Guerin* (2003) and *The Lord of the Rings* trilogy. In the UK, the film was sold as a political thriller as well as a costume drama. The trailer used dramatic choral and orchestral music, fast editing and close-ups to show the darkness closing in on

Elizabeth, and the posters emphasised the individuals in the story with a no-nonsense one word description for each:

Elizabeth HERETIC, Norfolk TRAITOR, Walsingham ASSASSIN, Robert Dudley LOVER

The American version of the poster used a colourful full length shot of the young Elizabeth, draped over a chair, showing her as sexual and confident woman, moving the emphasis away from political intrigue and choosing to sell the film as a doomed love story of sex and passion.

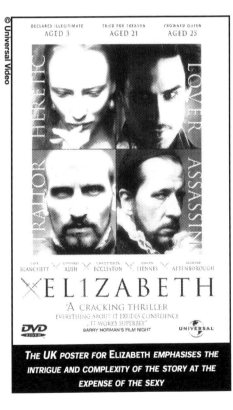

THE UK POSTER FOR ELIZABETH EMPHASISES THE INTRIGUE AND COMPLEXITY OF THE STORY AT THE EXPENSE OF THE SEXY

*Elizabeth* can also be studied with reference to two other British 'monarch movies' released during the 1990s, *The Madness of King George* and *Mrs Brown*. Problems relevant to the current Royal Family (relationships with the media, love versus duty, obsession with celebrity, relations between the State and the Church) are all present in the films and it would be interesting to examine them in detail.

# What does the film say? Film Language and Representation

As the title suggests, the film is centred on Elizabeth, the woman and the Queen. We follow the story from her point of view and are witness to her change in attitude and appearance as the film progresses.

The film gives a vivid sense of the feeling of the time, with the horror of the Protestant executions, the political machinations, the struggle for power, the colour and noise of the Elizabethan court and the threat of treachery towards the young Queen.

The film has many elements of a traditional 'historical' picture. The opening credit sequence with a written introduction placing the film in a historical context and the 'what happened then' end sequence; the costumes and dialogue; the use of British castles, country houses and gardens as settings, the *mise-en-scène* of the Tudor court scenes, arranged like Holbien paintings.

In aspects of music and camera work however, the film moves into political thriller territory – the subtly shot assassinations by Walsingham, the constant use of overhead shots (Norfolk striding through the dark halls of court, Elizabeth arriving at the Watergate after her arrest) where characters could be seen as pieces moving around a chessboard.

The main theme of the film is conflict. Conflict between Catholics and Protestants, between Mary and Elizabeth, between the Queen and her bishops, between love and duty. There is also a feeling of unease and danger that permeates the film, the sense that death is ever present. This dark and threatening feeling is put across in a number of ways. The horrific death of the martyrs in the opening sequence are shot from a high angle, with the audience looking down on the victims as they burn, a God's eye view of the event. The Duke of Norfolk, shaven headed, dressed in black (as all good cinema villains are!) is shown as a sexual and political predator.

The attempt by the monk, John Ballard, to kill Elizabeth is shot in the style of a horror film. He moves in slow motion, through the shadowy halls, his face covered by a cloak, and mysteriously vanishes when Elizabeth speaks.

*THE MISE-EN-SCÈNE OF HORROR: ELIZABETH AS A GENERIC HYBRID?*

However, it is Elizabeth who is central to the film. We first see her in the light, as a teenage girl, slowly dancing and smiling, free from affairs of state and responsibility. As the film goes on, we see her taking on more and more responsibility, shown in the change of her dress, make-up, hairstyle and bearing.

As she prepares to meet her bishops to discuss creating one Church of England, we see her preparing her speech as if she were an actress practising lines for a play, with short direct-to-camera pieces, edited together, almost looking like a video show-reel for an acting audition, emphasising the 'act' the Elizabeth has to initially put on for her court and her people. However, once she appears in front of the Bishops (the audience), she gains confidence and is shown gently berating her court with charm and wit.

*ELIZABETH REHEARSES HER ADDRESS TO THE BISHOPS, FILMED AND EDITED AS IF IT WERE AN ACTING AUDITION PIECE*

In the film's final sequence, we see her hair being shorn (linking her to the martyrs' deaths at the beginning of the film), with her sacrifice being love and marriage.
*'See, I have become a virgin. I am married to England'* she tells her ladies in waiting. The scene is shot almost as if it was showing Elizabeth's death (Mozart's mournful requiem mass on the soundtrack, white shrouds, her life flashing before her eyes) which of course it is – Elizabeth the woman is dead, reborn as Elizabeth the Queen.

Just as writers and artists through history have created many version of Queen Elizabeth (Good Queen Bess, Gloriana, the Virgin Queen, The Fairy Queen) so the film *Elizabeth* creates its own monarch – from eager teenager, besotted and in love with an older man through to the white-faced Queen of legend.

*'SEE, I HAVE BECOME A VIRGIN. I AM MARRIED TO ENGLAND'*

# THE HERITAGE FILM: FURTHER VIEWING

### MRS BROWN (1997)

*Directed by John Madden*
*Written by Jeremy Brock*

Slightly bizarre casting (Billy Connolly as John Brown) gives this BBC film an added dimension. The film is supposed to be about the relationship between the public and the Royal family in the late 19th century, but as with *The Madness of King George*, it can be read as a comment on the modern day monarchy. Judi Dench's portrayal of Queen Victoria can be compared with her later Oscar-winning turn as Queen Elizabeth in *Shakepeare in Love*.

### THE WINGS OF THE DOVE (1997)

*Directed by Iain Softley*
*Written by Hossein Amini, based on the novel by Henry James*

Coming on the wave of a brief series of Henry James' works (other adaptations were Jane Campion's *The Portrait of a Lady* (1996), Merchant-Ivory's *The Golden*

*Bowl* (2000) and Agneiska Holland's *Washington Square* (1997)), this was perhaps the best, an incisive examination of the destructive power of the privileged classes starring Helena Bonham Carter at her bohemian best.

## SHAKESPEARE IN LOVE (1998)
*Directed by John Madden*
*Written by Marc Norman and Tom Stoppard*
Massively successful US/UK co-production and an excellent example of how a major Hollywood company (in this case Miramax) can help a film gain an international profile through sheer panache and (allegedly) pushy marketing techniques at Oscar time.

## MANSFIELD PARK (2000)
*Written and directed by Patricia Rozema*
*Based on journals and the novel by Jane Austen*
Certainly a move away from the traditional Jane Austen adaptations from the BBC or on screen – for example Douglas McGrath's Quality Street version of *Emma* (1996) – Rozema brought in lesbian undertones, a sex scene only implied in the book and a hard hitting sequence bringing home the question of slavery, a practise prevalent at the time though ignored in other adaptations.

## I CAPTURE THE CASTLE (2003)
*Directed by Tim Fywell*
*Written by Heidi Thomas, based on the novel by Dodie Smith*
A refreshing and beautifully made film, from Dodie Smith's now cult novel, set in 1930s England and containing an excellent central performance by the young TV actress Romola Garai as the mainstay of the eccentric Mortmain family.

*An earlier version of this section appears on Film Education's National School Film Week website in the teacher's resource 'Representing History'.*

# Romantic Comedy: England, USA

**BRIDGET JONES'S DIARY (UK/USA 2001)**
*Director: by Sharon McGuire*
*Screenplay: Helen Fielding, Richard Curtis and Andrew*
*Davies, based on the novel by Helen Fielding*
*Music: Patrick Doyle*

**Bridget** ....................................Renée Zellweger
**Mark Darcy** ...........................Colin Firth
**Daniel Cleaver** .......................Hugh Grant
**Mr Jones** ................................Jim Broadbent
**Mrs Jones** ..............................Gemma Jones
**Jude** .......................................Shirley Henderson
**Shazza** ...................................Sally Phillips
**Tom** .......................................James Callis
**Natasha** ..................................Embeth Davidtz

**Released in the UK: April 2001**
**Budget: £14 million**
**UK box office: £42 million**

*Available to buy on Columbia Tri-Star DVD and video.*
*DVD includes directors commentary, deleted scenes,*
*Behind the Scenes featurette and music videos.*

## The film in context

*Bridget Jones's Diary* was based on the amazingly
popular book by Helen Fielding, itself derived from a
column in *The Independent* newspaper. The film was a
box office hit across the world and was another success
for the Working Title Company, which produced hits such
as *Four Wedding and A Funeral, Love Actually* and *Billy
Elliot*. Published in 1996, *Bridget Jones's Diary* didn't
initially become an instant best seller, only hitting the top
of the charts when it was published in paperback. It
centred on a world of thirty-something, professional
women worried about men, weight and drinking too
much, a world of Chardonnay and shagging where Colin

Firth as Mr Darcy in BBC's *Pride and Prejudice* was the national dreamboat (according to *Radio Times* readers, anyway).

Words like 'singleton' and 'fuck-wittage' became part of the language and the book launched the phenomenon of 'chick lit', a description dreamt up by the media that described popular, humorous novels written by women about women who worried about men, weight, etc.

Working Title optioned the book in 1997 and the company began casting the project. American Renée Zellweger was cast as Bridget and Colin Firth as Mark Darcy.

THE HEART OF DARCY: SELF REFLEXIVITY GOES MAD IN BRIDGET JONES'S DIARY AS COLIN FIRTH PLAYS MARK DARCY, BASED ON MR DARCY IN BBC'S PRIDE AND PREJUDICE, PLAYED BY...COLIN FIRTH

Hugh Grant starred as Daniel Cleaver, an interesting role in the fact that he is the less sympathetic character (compared to Mark) and somewhat of a diversion for Grant, by 2001 a massive worldwide star for playing mostly loveable, bumbling (a word the actor should really trademark for a nice line in regular income) Englishmen. Grant seems to have relished the role and it is a shame he hasn't been stretched in this direction more often. Only once before has he shown similar traits, in *An Awfully Big Adventure* (1994) based on the novel by Beryl Bainbridge, where he plays a manipulative theatre director who seduces a star-struck innocent (Georgina Cates).

Working Title have become a true phenomenon in the British film industry and are perhaps most recognised for their series of London based romantic comedies starring Hugh Grant and written by Richard Curtis, *Four Wedding and A Funeral, Notting Hill* and *Love Actually*. But as well as those trademark films, they have also helped to bring a number of US independent films to the screen including *Barton Fink* (1991), *Bob Roberts* (1992) and *O Brother, Where Art Thou* (2000) as well as producing 'smaller' British films such as the *Big Brother* horror-style film *My Little Eye* (2002) and the recent 'zomromcom' *Shaun Of the Dead*.

They are funded jointly by Hollywood's Universal Studios and StudioCanal in France, deals which guarantee them massive distribution clout across the US and Europe.

Tim Bevan, co-chairman of the company has stated:

*'Our films make a large contribution to the economy both in the making (UK spend or production) and in the receipts – both at the UK box office and through ancillary markets. Culturally our films are seen all around the world by millions of people and when British, represent British culture accordingly'.*[18]

Bevan's use of the phrase 'when British' is interesting as it acknowledges that Working Title don't always produce or co-produce 'British' films, which is explicitly the case in titles such as *Ned Kelly* (2003) and *High Fidelity* (2000).

The casting of Renée Zellweger as Bridget continues the tradition in the cycle of comedies from Working Title to use a Hollywood actress in key roles – Julia Roberts in *Notting Hill*, Andie Macdowell in *Four Weddings...* and Laura Linney in *Love Actually*. Zellweger doesn't play an American but the others do and apart from Roberts, the others don't actually *need* to be American; that is, their being American doesn't have anything to do with their characters. So, as well as being chosen for their acting skills, could it be that Universal Studios (who obviously have a major interest in Working Title's success as they co-fund it) insist on a American name in each film to help sell the film abroad? Kirstin Dunst is the latest import, starring alongside Paul Bettany in *Wimbledon* (2004).

Working Title's adaptation of Fielding's sequel, *Bridget Jones: The Edge of Reason* is set for release in the UK in November 2004...prepare for world domination once more.

## What does the film say? Film Language and representation

*Bridget Jones's Diary*, like most films based on popular novels, had an in-built audience for its release made up from lovers of the novel.

The image given from the posters, video covers and trailers was of a fast, funny, romantic comedy with Bridget shown as in the middle of a love triangle (quite literally on the posters) with Mark Darcy and Daniel Cleaver leaning in from each side. The two images used on the UK and US posters show the two sides of the character – on the UK image she is shown giggling, shyly hiding behind her diary, while on the US image, she has dropped the diary and confidently smiles at the camera, pencil in her mouth.

As in the novel, Bridget is shown as funny, warm, a person looking for love, susceptible to advances from lying cheating men. She can also be shallow and bitter (she believed Daniel's story of Mark's adultery without hesitation) and in her role as a working woman she is initially shown as pretty, vacuous and totally useless (her speech at the publishing launch party is disastrous as is her debut on UK TV sliding down a fireman's pole onto a camera). Much is made of Bridget's weight and lack of co-ordination – she collapses off a training bike in the gym and falls out of a taxi – and also her lack of tact and sophistication (her arrival at the supposed vicars and tarts party in her bunny suit, her terrible cooking experiments and her first introduction to Mark at her mother's house).

The idea is that the audience, as well as Mark, fall for her gradually and see her for herself – we love her 'just as she is'. Our sympathy for her is asked for from the very beginning of the film, in the opening sequence where her overbearing but well meaning mother tries to set her up at the Christmas party, her lecherous 'uncle' grabs her arse and Mark Darcy insults her within hearing distance. The film then cuts back to her flat with Bridget alone, finishing off a glass of wine in one gulp and smoking her way through repeats of *Frasier*. 'All By Myself' plays on the soundtrack, which Bridget mimes to perfectly, knowing the lyrics by heart and exactly when and where the instrumental breaks come in telling us this is an almost nightly occurrence.

'ALL BY MYSELF... DON'T WANNA BE...'

This opening sequence also tells us something about how Britain (and particularly England) will be shown in the film – there is snow falling at Christmas (deep, crunchy, clean snow) people live in picture postcard country houses and London streets are free from crime, beggars and litter. As with *Notting Hill*, where an 'ordinary' Englishman can meet, fall in love with (and have a family with) the biggest Hollywood actress in the world, *Bridget Jones's Diary* is unashamedly a fairytale, with Bridget's opening line 'It all began on New Year's Day..' spoken against a magical music motif that tells us none of this is supposed to be real.

However, Bridget is constantly shown as a 'real' woman, vacuuming smoking a cigarette, desperately trying to squeeze into big knickers, falling out a of a taxi drunk. She is an 'everywoman' that the majority of the audience can identify with and therefore care about. Her world, although seemingly glamorous (a London publishing company, dahhhling!), is also the world of dreadful daytime TV, getting drunk with your mates, being cheated on and hoping your boyfriend will take you on a mini-break.

Much was made of the fact that Renée Zellweger put on weight for the role and also worked incognito in a London publishing company to get her accent and language right. In acting terms, this is the area of the Method – shades of Robert De Niro gaining weight for *Raging Bull* (1980) – and the stories aim to give the film a credibility – the actress is trying to 'become' Bridget. These stories were possibly emphasisd to deflect consternation from the press and public about the use of an American star playing such a well loved English character.[19]

Zellweger builds on the comedic roles she had in *Jerry McGuire* (1996) and more particularly *Nurse Betty* (2000), where she plays a character similar to Bridget (slightly kooky 30-something, looking for love) who mistakes reality for fantasy in a US soap opera. *Bridget Jones's Diary* certainly made her name in the UK and sealed her reputation in the US – she was Oscar nominated for the role, again for *Chicago* (2002) and won for *Cold Mountain* (2003).

## The Romantic Comedy: Further Viewing

### SHOOTING FISH (1997)
*Directed by Stefan Schwartz*
*Written by Stefan Schwartz and Richard Holmes*
Quirky and enjoyable film, one of the first funded by the National Lottery and now often overlooked in the wake of Working Title's series of massively popular comedies. Elements of romance, farce and an upbeat cast combined with a quirky Britpop soundtrack.

## SLIDING DOORS (1998)

*Written and directed by Peter Howitt*

A UK 'high concept' film – meaning that only a very simple pitch is needed to tell the story. Girl misses tube train and splits into two, and we follow each personality... one who catches the train, one who misses it. Gwyneth Paltrow does a good job with the English accent, but John Hannah perhaps relies too much on his cheery *Four Weddings...* persona. For a British comedy, pretty tragic at the end (for one of Gwyneth's characters, anyway).

## THIS YEAR'S LOVE (1998)

*Written and directed by David Kane*

Set in a bustling Camden, this is a witty comedy of sexual manners, with an excellent cast, most notably Kathy Burke, and Jennifer Ehle playing against type as a grungy hippie chick out for kicks.

## NOTTING HILL (1998)

*Directed by Roger Michell*
*Written by Richard Curtis*

Criticised at the time of release by some critics for it's 'whitening' of Notting Hill (there is not a black character in any leading role in a film set in the home of one of world's biggest Afro-Caribbean carnivals), the film is perhaps interesting to look at in terms of stardom and fame with stars Julia Roberts and Hugh Grant moving into mega-status at the time of release. It's actually a fairy tale, pure and simple, and says a lot more about Hollywood than West London.

## LOVE ACTUALLY (2003)

*Written and directed by Richard Curtis*

The latest release from the Working Title/Richard Curtis/Hugh Grant stable, this again proved a massive success in the UK and the US, but with perhaps Curtis overdoing the narrative somewhat, with around ten stories of love and lust happening at once. By far the best performance (apart from Emma Thompson who is powerfully touching) is from Hugh Grant in the DVD commentary, as he makes wonderfully dry comments throughout about Colin Firth's hair and Curtis' directing style.

# Social Realism: From the Roots

**SWEET SIXTEEN (UK/Germany/Spain/France/Italy 2002)**
*Director: Ken Loach*
*Screenplay: Paul Laverty*
*Music: George Fenton*

**Liam** .........................................Martin Compstone
**Chantelle** ...............................Annmarie Fulton
**Pinball**...................................William Ruane
**Suzanne** ................................Michelle Abercromby
**Stan** .........................................Gary McCormick
**Jean** .........................................Michelle Coulter
**Rab** .........................................Tommy McKee

**Released in the UK : October 2002**
**Budget: £2.4 million**
**UK box office: £825,000**

*Available to buy on Icon video and DVD.*
*DVD features Ken Loach commentary, BBC*
*documentary, outtakes, trailers.*

## The film in context

*Sweet Sixteen* can be seen as a return to Loach's roots after the international politics of *Bread and Roses* (2000) set in LA and looking at immigrant workers rights, *Carla's Song* (1996) a love story based around Nicaraguan freedom fighters, and *Land and Freedom* (1995), a powerful look back at the Spanish Civil War.

Though it is set closer to home (Glasgow), the film is no less political than those titles. Again written by his collaborator Paul Laverty, the film won accolades across the world, winning Best Screenplay at Cannes in 2002 and actor Martin Compstone (who plays Liam) was up for the Best Actor award.

Set around the housing estates of Greenock and Port Glasgow at the mouth of the Clyde, *Sweet Sixteen* was shot on location and Loach used many local people in small roles in the film recruited from community centres and employment training courses.

Loach has a record of portraying the working-class cultures of Britain with a raw and immediate power. Largely improvised dialogue, location shooting, handheld camera work, use of non-actors in small roles, a socialist agenda and an anti-authoritaty tone are all hallmarks of Loach's work, beginning with his earlier television work such as *Up the Junction* (1965). His films have been set in many different areas of Britain (London, the North West, West Yorkshire, Scotland) and his influence can not only be seen in cinema, particularly with the work of Shane Meadows, but on television dramas such as *Clocking Off* and *Shameless*. Even comedies such as *The Office* and *The Royle Family* owe an allegiance to Loach in their visual style (camera work, settings and naturalistic acting) and characters.

The hard-hitting subject matter and the swearing caused the film to get an '18' certificate for cinema and video release, meaning the very audience that were likely to gain the most from watching the film couldn't see it. The decision infuriated Loach, confirming his disgust for the nanny state begun by the Tories and sustained by New Labour.[20]

Also obviously influenced by Loach's work was *The Full Monty* which covers many topics in its narrative that are familiar Loach areas (unemployment, loss of traditional masculine roles, family break-ups, destruction of working class communities). However, possibly as it had an eye on the international market, particularly America (it was financed and distributed by US giant 20th Century Fox), *The Full Monty* is played strictly as a comedy, with little or no explicit social comment or genuine feeling for the area and people who live there – few of the cast were local for example, or even from Yorkshire.

In the current film-making climate, only Amber Films, based in Newcastle upon Tyne, can claim to produce films that portray the working class and their culture in a way that Loach attempts. With Amber's features and shorts, both fiction and documentary, they integrate with the North East communities, involving them in casting and scripting. As with Loach, traditional industries (fishing, mining, farming) are treated with a dignity and respect perhaps lacking in the more popular cinematic representations.

## What does the film say? Film Language and Representation

As in *Cathy Come Home* (1965), *Kes* (1969), *Raining Stones* and *Ladybird Ladybird* (1994) Loach examines how dysfunctional family life, poverty and outside influences can shatter the family unit. The main character Liam is never shown as a clichéd 'bad lad' – what he does, he does for good reasons and he is shown as being part way between being child and adult, but needing to make adult decisions that will change his life.

Although he is involved in drug running, stealing and becomes caught up in a horrendously brutal act near the end of the film, he is also shown as the strong and noble member of the family. His mother is weak and throws his kindness back in his face, his best friend sells him out and his grandfather has no time for him.

He is constantly striving for a better world, where there's 'nae drugs and nae polis' and just wants to make a home for himself and his mother. Meeting her from jail, Liam stands proudly in his suit and tie – he *has* grown up into a man but when he loses her again, he flies into a rage against his sister and moves across to 'the dark side' of town with Stan (his mother's violent boyfriend) and his grandfather.

Seeing the destruction drugs have done to his family, Liam nonetheless uses them as a way to get money to buy his dream home. He is beaten by a gang, loses his caravan and his best friend and by the end of the film possibly loses his own freedom. The final sequence showing Liam

NOT A 'BAD LAD': LIAM IS PLEASED TO SEE HIS MUM IN SWEET SIXTEEN

wandering by the river in a daze doesn't give us a tidy happy ending (another Loach trademark) as we realise that for the crime he has done, he will be treated as an adult rather than a child as he is now 'sweet sixteen'.

The use of location, the language and accents, the acting styles and the camera work all combine to give the film an almost documentary style and the occasional use of music on the soundtrack comes almost as a surprise as it seems to break the spell that we are watching real life.

Loach uses the locations and props in a sometimes surprising way, which gives us unexpected images of beauty (a rainbow over the industrial landscape of the Clyde, a caravan that is seen as a palace – 'a couple a' hens, a couple a' cans…paradise man', says Liam as he settles down with Pinball inside).

There is also a strong streak of humour running through the film. Liam and Pinball are like Butch and Sundance as they steal Liam's grandfather's teeth then his drugs stash, and watch the reaction with glee from an opposite tower block. The use of a health club as a front for a drugs ring is nicely ironic and Liam's retort of 'Laughing at your bosses jokes?' when he is asked by the local Mr

Big if he knows what initiative is, is delivered with the timing of a born comedian.

There is also a wonderful throwaway line as Liam is looking to make a drugs deal in an unfamiliar part of town and asks someone 'is there any place round here where the junkies stand?' with the nonchalance of a tourist asking the way to the Glasgow Film Theatre.

We are asked to identify with Liam before the film even starts – the theatrical poster shows a large image of a smiling, cheeky Liam, looking like any other British teenager. Audiences are reminded of that other great Ken Loach teenager, Billy Casper in *Kes*, and Liam certainly has a similar defiance and strength of character.

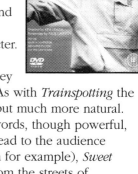

The use of language is also a key element of the film's strength. As with *Trainspotting* the Scottish dialect is very strong, but much more natural. Whereas in *Trainspotting* the words, though powerful, feel as though they are being read to the audience (Renton's *'Choose life...'* speech for example), *Sweet Sixteen*'s language is straight from the streets of Greenock – it takes time for English speaking audiences to get used to the dialect and the phrasing.[21]

As with all of Ken Loach's films, but particularly those which deal with the British working class, from *Cathy Come Home* onwards, the technique of the drama-documentary is used to give his films a sense of the real – they are realistic in the sense that they are shot on location, use non-actors in some roles, have characters that speak in that region's accent and dialect, and constantly blur the line between fact and fiction. Although *Sweet Sixteen* is just as much a work of cinematic fiction as, say, *Billy Elliot*, it is the techniques mentioned above that allow Loach's film to feel more 'real' and therefore, to audiences, more memorable.[22]

# SOCIAL REALISM: FURTHER VIEWING

### NIL BY MOUTH (1997)
*Written and directed by Gary Oldman*
An unsparing account of the devastation alcohol and violence can have on a family, based on Oldman's own upbringing. Kathy Burke and Ray Winstone shine and it is all as far away from *Eastenders* as you can get.

### THE SCAR (1997)
*Written and directed by the Amber Production team*
Set in the coalfields of East Durham, Amber's powerful drama stars Charlie Hardwick as the ex-wife of a miner who falls for the new open cast mine manager (Bill Speed). Wonderfully observed, with an honesty and genuine feel for the landscape missing in more successful films such as *Billy Elliot*.

### THE WAR ZONE (1998)
*Directed by Tim Roth*
*Written by Alexander Stuart, based on his novel*
A low key directorial debut about a father's abuse of his daughter from actor Roth, the film has a moving central performance by Lara Belmont and Ray Winstone is frighteningly persuasive as the father. A difficult but rewarding piece of work.

### THE LAST RESORT (2000)
*Directed by Pawel Pawlikowski*
*Written by Pawel Pawlikowski and Rowan Joffe*
An original take on the Romeo and Juliet story as a young Russian asylum seeker, Tanya, is left alone in Britain with her young son and meets local lad Alfie at an out-of-season seaside resort. Still highly relevant today, the film could be watched in relation to other recent dramas centring on asylum seekers such as Stephen Frears' *Dirty Pretty Things* (2002) and Michael Winterbottom's *In This World*.

## ALL OR NOTHING (2002)

*Written and directed by Mike Leigh*

Incisive study of a family barely able to communicate with one another verbally, but where looks, glances and expressions can speak volumes. Lesley Manville and Timothy Spall shine as the married couple with Leigh again finding magic among the working classes.

# British Asian Cinema: Eastern Approaches

### BEND IT LIKE BECKHAM (UK/Germany 2002)

*Director: Gurinder Chadha*
*Screenplay: Gurinder Chadha, Paul Mayeda Berges and Guljit Bindra*
*Music: Craig Pruess*
Songs include: *Move On Up* (Curtis Mayfield); *The Power Of Love* (Amar); *Independence Day* (Melanie C); *Dream The Dream* (Shaznay Lewis); *Inner Smile* (Texas); *I Wish* (Victoria Beckham); *Jind Mahi* (Malkit Singh); *My Final Peace* (Gunjan)

**Jesminder Bhamra**...............Parminda Nagra
**Jules Paxton** ...........................Keira Knightley
**Joe** .............................................Jonathon Rhys-Meyers
**Mr Bhamra**.............................Anupam Kher
**Mrs Bhamra**...........................Shaleen Khan
**Pinky Bhamra** .......................Archie Panjabi
**Alan Paxton** ...........................Frank Harper
**Paula Paxton** ........................Juliet Stevenson
**Mel**.............................................Shaznay Lewis
**Tony**.........................................Ameet Chana
**Teetu** .......................................Kulvinder Ghir
**Meena** .....................................Pooja Shah
**Bubbly** ....................................Paven Virk
**Monica**....................................Preeya Kalidas
**Themselves**............................John Motson
.................................................John Barnes
.................................................Gary Lineker
.................................................Alan Hanson

**Available on VHS (Warner Home Video) and DVD. DVD includes commentary from Gurinder Chada, a behind the scenes documentary, the *Hot Hot Hot* video, 10 deleted scenes and a recipe for Aloo Gobi.**

# The film in context

*Bend It Like Beckham* was one of the surprise hits of 2002, taking over £11,000,000 at the UK box office and striking a chord with a range of audiences at cinemas. A vibrant and colourful British comedy about a young girl from a Sikh family who desperately wants to play football against the wishes of her traditional parents, the film can be seen to follow the path of other recent British Asian films such as *Bhaji On the Beach*, *Anita and Me* and *East Is East* in its examination of culture clashes and family traditions.

*Bend It Like Beckham* takes these themes and adds extra ingredients to the dish – football, Shakespearean confusions over identity and sexuality, in-jokes about both British pop culture and the Sikh way of life, and a music soundtrack mixing a range of East/West sounds and musical styles.

It's also useful to look at *Bend It Like Beckham* within a wider context of the British Asian experience in popular culture and media, such as the portrayal of Asian culture on TV including *Ali G, Goodness Gracious Me*, characters in soaps such as *Coronation Street* and *Eastenders* – even a recent Walkers Crisps advert had Gary Lineker appearing in a mini-Bollywood musical — and the Asian language, music and fashion that has now flowed into the mainstream.

In terms of UK cinema audiences, the key demographic or target group for the film on its release was teenagers and twenty-somethings (approximately 12 to 25 year olds), aiming particularly at the female market.

Given the rise in interest in football amongst young women in terms of the growth of women's football clubs, more women watching the game and the recent phenomenon of international players as superstar pin-ups (David Beckham, David Ginola, Robert Pires, etc.), it was thought there was an untapped female audience for a movie about football that had two strong female central characters.

In tabloid film magazine language, it could be seen as both a 'chick flick' and a 'date movie' with its mixture of football, comedy, romance and a young attractive cast appealing to both male and female audiences.

The film's release in April 2002 also benefited from the media interest leading up to the World Cup in Japan, and coincided with the frenzy around David Beckham's toe, which could not help but assist the film.

The UK poster and adverts emphasise the comedy aspects of the film over the sport (bright colours, smiling faces, press quotes such as 'you'll be grinning from ear to ear', 'hilariously fresh' and 'the best British comedy since *Bridget Jones's Diary*'.

The tagline on the poster, 'Who wants to cook Aloo Gobi when you can bend a ball like Beckham?' sums up the dilemma of Jess in one line, playing her Punjabi traditions against her new British identity.

## What does the film say? Film Language and Representation

The film explores a numbers of themes and gives us two main areas of study in terms of representation: gender and the British Asian experience. These two areas can be brought together by looking at the main protagonists, Jess and Jules, their respective families, and the issues explored.

Jess is the central character and we follow the story through her experiences. She is shown as an intelligent young woman, with three A Levels, who tries to be a 'good' girl for her mother and father, who is also passionate about playing football. But her rebellious streak is not aimed to hurt her parents. Jess has already started to move away from traditional ways (her name is westernised from Jesminder) and her family think that football will have a corrupting influence – 'showing your bare legs to the boys' says her mother.

**WHEN WORLDS COLLIDE: JESS AMIDST THE ICONOGRAPHY OF BRITISH FOOTBALL CULTURE**

Our first sight of Jess is actually in a fantasy sequence, playing for Manchester United and scoring the winning goal, and then we see her in her room, surrounded by icons traditionally linked to boys (football scarves, posters, wearing a Manchester United top). Jess is seemingly not bothered by her appearance and is not interested in 'typical' teenage girl activities (shopping, boys, make-up, clothes, pop music). When her mother finally gets her into the kitchen to learn to cook a traditional Indian meal, Jess is seen playing keepy-uppy with various vegetables.

She only becomes aware of her femininity when she gets to know Joe and begins to change (literally in Hamburg, when Jules dresses her up for the party and does her hair).

Jules complements Jess in a number of ways – their names are similar, both want to play football, both have trouble from their mothers. Like Jess, Jules is shown to be ambitious but at least has the backing of her father. Her mother, just like Mrs Bharmra, wants her daughter to be more 'traditional', trying to stop her buying a sports bra and worried that her obsession with football is making her 'less feminine'.

Jess's family and background are explored in a number of ways and emphasise the bringing together of the traditional and the modern in contemporary British Asian life. The picture of the Holy Man on the wall of the front room, the costumes and greetings and the disapproval of marriage outside the community are contrasted with the modern thinking of characters like Jess, and also Tony, who is planning to tell his mother he is gay.

Tony is shown as a positive character who acts in a 'decent' manner towards Jess, pretending he wants to marry her so she can go to America to play football. Jess understands and accepts Tony's gayness, but we never learn what happens when Tony comes out to his more macho male friends and his more traditional family.

Jules and Jess's suspected 'lesbian' relationship is handled with humour – Jules's Mum is shown as being totally over the top in her condemnation then calming down when she learns the truth, admitting she was always a fan of Martina Navratilova.

The traditional vs. modern conflict is interestingly not just shown as an older vs. young generation dispute. Jess's sister Pinky is just as traditional in her outlook as her mother – 'Don't you want all this?' she asks Jess on her wedding day, and Mr Bharmra is shown to be sympathetic and understanding of Jess's point of view.

Racism is touched on both in terms of institutionalised racism (Mr Bharmra was not let into his local cricket club due to membership rules) and more directly, when Jess is called a Paki by an opposing player. The football coach, Joe, is Irish, and sympathises with Jess, implying that he also has experienced racism from the English.

Unlike a film such as *My Beautiful Laundrette*, an exploration of racism is not *Bend It Like Beckham*'s main theme or concern. Overall, the Asian community is shown as both retaining their traditions and culture but integrating successfully into some aspects of British life.

Although the film could fall within a number of areas (teen movie, sports movie), it is essentially a comedy centred on the British Asian community and there are number of comic traditions and situations used:

- *Culture clash* – Always a rich seam for comedy, the film not only looks at the differences between the British and Asian lifestyles, but also the clashes within the Punjabi community itself.

British people trying to 'get' the Asian culture are gently mocked, particularly when Jess arrives to see Jules. Mrs Paxton welcomed her with a feeble 'Oooh, I made a lovely curry yesterday' and tells her that her mum will obviously be 'fixing her up with a nice handsome doctor'.

Joe arrives at Jess's house to explain about the crucial match and Pinky, Jess's sister, asks why she's brought home a 'Gora' (slang for a white person). 'He's Irish,' says Jess, to which Pinky replies, 'Yeah, well they all look the bloody same', which turns the traditional stereotype on its head.

- *Sight gags* – Used in cinema from the silent days onwards, *Bend It Like Beckham* utilises them to heighten the comedy, particularly at the expense of Jess' older relatives. A mobile phone rings in the front room and ten elderly Punjabi women rummage in their bags to answer. These characters reappear when Jess has to take a crucial free kick and she imagines the opposition wall has become four of her relatives plus her pleading sister.

- *Comic misunderstandings* – The film is rife with misunderstandings and confusions which come to a head at Pinky's wedding. Through a series of misheard conversations and wrong assumptions, Mrs Paxton thinks Jules and Jess are lovers, and while in the early part of the film she makes a joke out of it, telling Jules 'There's a reason why Sporty Spice is the only one without a fella', she becomes increasingly distressed about the situation.

'GET YOUR LESBIAN FEET OUT OF MY SHOES!'

Confronting Jess at the wedding, Mrs Paxton accuses her of being 'all respectful here with your lot' and finally shouts 'get your lesbian feet out of my shoes!', shoes which Jules had lent Jess earlier.

This also provides some comic lines of dialogue, again from the confused elderly relatives – 'I thought she was a Pisces'… 'She's not Lebanese, she's Punjabi!'

## A Note on Bollywood
'Bollywood' is a term used by journalists, film-makers and the media to describe films from the Indian film industry and mainly consisting of large scale popular musicals produced for national and international

consumption. The name comes from combining Hollywood and Bombay, the city which is the centre of the Indian film industry and the films are usually a mixture of colourful romance, comedy and family drama, with sometimes up to a dozen musical sequences.

Many films have been released in the UK, usually in Hindi, but not always with English subtitles.

There are two very useful articles available from the British Film Institute about the genre – 'Hooray for Bollywood' and 'Bollywood and Beyond: Teaching Indian Cinema'. Check www.bfi.org and click on 'education' for details.

An earlier version of this section appears on Film Education's National Schools Film Week website, under *Bend It Like Beckham*: A Teachers' Resource.

# The British Asian Film: Further Viewing

### BHAJI ON THE BEACH (1993)
*Directed by Gurinder Chadha*
*Written by Meera Syal*
A comedy in the Ealing style, exploring the racial and generational problems that follow a Birmingham Asian Women's group as they have a day trip to Blackpool.

### EAST IS EAST (1999)
*Directed by Damian O' Donnell*
*Written by Ayub Khan-Din, based on his play*
Set in Salford in the 1970s, on the surface this is a comedy of manners seen through the eyes of the youngest son in the family, but the film has a darker side exploring domestic violence and physical and mental abuse.

### ANITA AND ME (2002)
*Directed by Metin Huseyin*
*Written by Meera Syal, based on her novel*
Set in a 1970s Midlands town, the film centres on 12 year old Indian girl Meena and her friendship with the blonde, glamorous 14 year old Anita and her dysfunctional family.

## BOLLYWOOD QUEEN (2003)

*Directed by Jeremy Wooding*
*Written by Neil Spence, based on* Romeo and Juliet *by William Shakespeare*
Exhuberant Hindi musical romance mixing Bollywood with the UK club scene, as an Indian girl falls for an English boy and they have to love across the great divide. Not quite as epic as some Bollywood musicals (this is 90 minutes rather than 3 hours) the film would be a good introduction to the themes and conventions of an Indian musical.

## BRIDE AND PREJUDICE (2004)

*Directed by Gurinder Chadha*
*Written by Gurinder Chadha and Paul Mayeda Berges, based on the novel by Jane Austen*
Jane Austen meets Bollywood – Gurinder Chadha's colourful take on the classic novel. Another film version has been announced, produced by Working Title films, and starring Keira Knightley as Elizabeth Bennet.

Box office data for all the films in this chapter from *Producing the Goods? UK Film Production since 1991* (Phil Wickham, BFI Library Information Services, London 2003).

# Notes

1. Barr, Charles, *English Hitchcock* (Cameron and Hollis: Moffat, 1999).

2. Robert Murphy in his written introduction to his session, *Why British Cinema?*, Bradford Media Studies Conference, November 2003.

3. I promised myself not to refer to *Carry On* films in this Guide, but just couldn't resist here.

4. A couple of things to bear in mind when reading lists or articles about how well a film has done at the box office – the income from films from the early to mid 90s will probably not be adjusted for cheaper tickets (i.e. a cinema ticket in 1993 was a lot cheaper than a ticket in 2004). Also, London prices tend to distort levels of box office income, as tickets for say, large West End cinemas could be in the region of £8–£10, compared with £5–6 for the rest of the country.

5. Street, Sarah, *British National Cinema* (see bibliography).

6. The simple economics are 'not many people want to see foreign films, so fewer are shown'. This circular argument is also true for terrestrial television channels – 'we don't put foreign language films on BBC1 as they won't be popular'. However, surely the more chances people get to see and enjoy subtitled films, the more they will seek them out in the future...?

   We also see the realities of supply and demand in retail, where foreign language films and silent cinema videos and DVDs are rarely dropped in price to the level of Hollywood blockbusters.

7. One of British cinema's most influential and controversial films, *Performance* was completed in 1968 but not released until 1970. It was re-released in the UK by the BFI in 2004.

8. Attendances at British cinemas had fallen to 116 million by 1975.

9. Blur just shaved it with *Country House* but Oasis got their own back with the multi-million selling *Definitely Maybe* album...and the North shall rise again!

10. From 'Underbelly UK: The 1990s Underclass Film, Masculinity and the Ideologies of New Britain', Claire Monk in *British Cinema, Past and Present* (see bibliography).

11. *The Full Monty* was incredibly successful at the UK box office (£52.2 million) beating recent hits such as *Four Weddings and a Funeral* (£27.7 million), *Billy Elliot* (£18 million) and *Notting Hill* (£31 million), and part of that can certainly be put down to its marketing and its wide ranging appeal to men and women (bloke-ish humour + chick flick laughs). However, one factor may also have helped – the tragic death of Princess Diana in August 1997, which occurred just before the film's release in the UK and may have created an audience for a feel-good British comedy.

12. In the US, *Brassed Off* was marketed as a jolly romantic comedy much to the consternation of some American viewers (see the Internet Movie Database – imdb.com – entry for the film which has the original US poster/video box image and discussions from fans).

13. Figures taken from *Producing the Goods?* and the UKFC website.

14. To discover what Peter Greenaway is doing now, visit his website at www.tulselupernetwork.com.

15. 'Fury as Lottery Money Funds Vile Sex Film' was a typical headline from the *Daily Mail* from 21 February, 2004. Concentrating on *Sex Lives Of the Potato Men* starring Mackenzie Crook and Jonny Vegas, the article basically consisted of a scathing review by Christopher Tookey, the paper's film critic, and some quotes from Anne Widdicombe MP and a right wing evangelical Christian Internet pastor from the US, Dr Adrian Rogers, neither of whom had seen the film.

16. One interesting aspect of the City Screen circuit is they are currently championing the use of digital films screening via computer as the way forward for cinema exhibition and distribution. A preview screening of Peter Greenaway's **Tulse Luper Suitcases** at the City Screen site in Cambridge in July 2003 offered a demonstration. The company equipping the cinema is called Arts Alliance Media, part of the Arts Alliance Group that owns a large share of...City Screen.

17. *Whale Rider* and *Goodbye Lenin* both took around £1 million at the UK box office (figures from the Internet Movie Database).

18. Minutes of evidence from Tim Bevan, Working Title Films, from the Select Committee report on Culture, Media and Sport, 2 April 2003.

19. Still, we sent Vivien Leigh to play a much loved and typically American character in *Gone with the Wind* (1939) and anyway, Zellweger is actually very good in the movie.

20. The council in Greenock where the film was shot overturned the BBFC rating and gave it a '15', thus allowing Martin Compstone, the star, to actually watch it.

21. When the film was released in the UK in October 2002, there was talk of some prints having subtitles put onto the first reel (around 20 minutes of screen time) to gradually wean audiences into the language. Whether this actually happened is unconfirmed.

22. One of the most perceptive and sensitive reviews of the film is, perhaps surprisingly, on the US right wing *Christian Spotlight on the Movies* website on www.christiananswers.net/spotlight/movies. However, just to keep the balance, they also attack *The Wizard of Oz* (1939) for containing 'overt witchcraft' and *Scooby Doo* (2002) for containing references to Satanism and Buddhism (?!) and having a 'heavy emphasis on voodoo'.

# Glossary of Useful Terms

**Art house**
Thought by some cinema marketing officers as either a term of abuse or the kiss of death for audiences, it's nonetheless a useful term describing a cinema that shows a range of films, including foreign language, US/UK independent work and old films, or a noun describing a particular film that falls in those categories.

**Box office take**
The amount paid of the counter at cinemas for particular films on current release.

**Brit.pack**
Used since the late 1980s to describe any young up and coming group of British cinema actors, writers or directors who have made a mark internationally. Current group could include Keira Knightly and Orlando Bloom, for example.

**Brit.lit**
Used to describe the cycle of costume dramas and English literature adaptations prevelant since the early-to-late 1990s.

**Brit.grit**
As above but used for working-class dramas or crime films usually set in an urban centre.

**Co-production**
A British film that may have some funding from another

source, usually the USA or elsewhere in Europe.

## Cross-over
A film that the distributor thinks has appeal both to the discerning art house crowd (so it may be screened in some independent cinemas) as well as some of the general population (so it may be in some multiplex chains). Recent examples are *Girl with a Pearl Earring* and *Nicholas Nickleby* (2002).

## Distribution
The process of sending a film out to audiences via cinemas and publicising it through variable sized marketing campaigns.

## Exhibition
The process of showing a film to an audience, usually in a cinema but also in other settings such as community centres, film societies and schools.

## Megaplex
A huge cinema complex, with over 20 screens, as well as bars, resteraunts and other leisure outlets. Britain's first, Warner's Star City in Birmingham, now houses the UK's biggest casino.

## Multiplex
The cinema system that revolutionised cinema-going in the UK in the mid-1980s which basically did to cinema what the Americans did with fast food shops – made them look all the same, offered the same thing in each, taught staff to use American phrases like 'regular' instead of medium sized and told the public they were getting 'choice'.

## Print
The copy of the film that is sent out to cinemas – each copy can cost up to £2000 to make. Films are still sent out from depots via train or lorry and carried upstairs to projection booths by weary projectionists. Screening films 'down the line' digitally is still a long way off as the process of blowing up a film image sourced from

computer disc to cinema screen size is still a problem.

## Regional Film Theatre (RFT)
A rarely used name for an independent, subsidised cinema that screens a range of World Cinema (both classic and contemporary) and which has education about, and understanding of, cinema in all its forms at the heart of its remit.

*See EXHIBITION section above for more details.*

## Repertory
Films screened from throughout cinema history, maybe as part of a double bill or forming part of a retrospective or special season at an RFT or other independent cinema.

## Specialised film
A UKFC definition that describes any films that are in the main not blockbuster/mainstream/commercial major Hollywood studio backed (i.e. foreign language, classics, repertory, archive, documentaries, short films, avant-garde/experimental).

## Three day gross
The most important three days in a film's life – the Friday, Saturday and Sunday of the opening weekend of a movie and the money it takes at the box office can decide the fate of the film, its producers and (sometimes) its stars. More and more blockbuster films are having Thursday paid previews to bolster the opening weekend figures – in the case of the *The Lord Of The Rings* trilogy, the previews began on Wednesdays.

## Zomromcom
A term specifically created for the new British film *Shaun of the Dead*, which is a romantic comedy – with zombies in it.

# Access to British Films

## DVD or VHS?

Most of the films mentioned in this Guide will be available on either DVD or VHS at any high street store. I've found **HMV** and **Virgin** to be the best (also **Tower Records** if you are lucky enough to have one) and both shops have constant sales with some excellent bargains. Films on VHS are now extremely cheap (usually £2.99–£5.99) for most titles except new releases, and DVD are getting cheaper by the month which is important if you have restricted budgets and want to build a library.

If you are finding it difficult to track down a particular title, you will probably find it via the **Movie Mail** mail order company at PO Box 220, Hereford, HR4 OWW Tel: (0870) 264 9000  www.moviemail-online.co.uk

They produce regular monthly newsletters and an excellent glossy annual brochure with all titles available including features, documentaries, shorts packages and non-fiction.

The BFI also has an extensive list of films available to buy or rent (on DVD or VHS) including foreign language film, classics and silent cinema. Go to their website for details.

# In the Cinema

To see the widest range of new British films, you really need to juggle between visiting your local multiplex and your local independent art house cinema. Your local multiplex is easy to find (check out each of their websites or look in the local paper). Here you will see UK films such as *Love Actually* and *Shaun of the Dead*, the James Bonds and the Harry Potters. You may also briefly see the more art house titles such as *Girl with a Pearl Earring* and *Touching the Void*.

To seek out your nearest art house cinema (where you may see re-released classics, older films as part of seasons, titles screened as part of a tour or new British non-mainstream films) there is either the commercial City Screen circuit (on www.picturehouses.co.uk) or the non-profit making Regional Film Theatres, who provide regular school screenings, programme notes and an enthusiastic and knowledgable staff (www.bfi.org.uk/showing/regionnal/index.html).

# Bibliography

## Books

The following list includes books I've found particularly useful as I've been working on this guide but is not an extensive list of texts that refer to British cinema. For a detailed bibliography see the list compiled by Jane Bryan in *British Cinema Past and Present* (below).

Asby, Justine and Higson, Andrew (eds), *British Cinema Past and Present*, Routledge: London, 2000.

Cattarall, Ali and Wells, Simon (eds), *Your Face Here – British Cult Movies Since the Sixties*, Fourth Estate: London, 2002.
Of particular interest are the last two chapters on *Trainspotting* and *Lock, Stock and Two Smoking Barrels*.

Monk, Clare and Sargeant, Amy (eds), *British Historical Cinema: The History, Heritage and Costume Film*, Routledge: London, 2002.
This title is part of the excellent *British Popular Cinema* series with other titles including *British Crime Cinema* (eds Steve Chibnall and Robert Murphy); *British Science Fiction Cinema* (ed. I.Q. Hunter) and *British Horror Cinema* (eds Steve Chibnall and Julian Petley).

Murphy, Robert (ed.), *British Cinema of the 90s*, BFI Publishing: London, 2000.

Murphy, Robert (ed.), *The British Cinema Book*, BFI Publishing: London, 1997 (second edition 2001).

Street, Sarah, *British National Cinema*, Routledge: London, 1997.

# Journals

*The Journal of Popular British Cinema* was an extremely useful publication which began in 1998 and ran for 5 issues, covering a range of topics relevant to British cinema from the silent days up to current titles. Published by the Society for the study of Popular British Cinema, it has now transformed into *The Journal of British Cinema and Television*, published by Edinburgh University Press (EUP). Copies can be ordered via the EUP website at www.eup.ed.ac.uk

# Key publications

Some works that may be useful when looking at recent trends and developments in the British film industry are:

*The UK Film Council: Three Years On* (UKFC 2003)
Very useful to give an overview of the many different facets of Film Council work and funding strands. However, be warned, as it's published by the UKFC itself, is not a critical document and is written in consultant-speak full of 'initiatives' and 'strategies'. Available from the UKFC.

*Film in the UK 2002 Statistical Handbook* (UKFC 2003)
Full of facts and figures about UK film production during 2002, with box office information, how UK films have done abroad, sales of DVD and videos and how the UK film and media workforce is made up. Available from UKFC.

*Producing the Goods? UK Film Production since 1991 - An Information Briefing:* Phil Wickham (BFI Library Information Services, 2003)
A fascinating look at the production and box office success (and otherwise) of British productions (and co-productions), with a useful narrative section covering trends and developments and an extensive list of titles, their budgets and their UK box office takings. Available

from the BFI Library Information Department.

*In the Picture* (published three times a year)
An excellent resource for teachers to learn about the latest trends in film and media education. The magazine covers all areas of media study but has reviews and analysis of new films, new publications, and information on film screenings and events across the country. For more information visit www.itpmag.demon.uk.

# Useful
# Websites

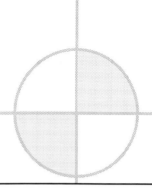

**BRITISH BOARD OF FILM CLASSIFICATION**
**www.bbfc.co.uk**
A fascinating look at how this elusive body decides what films we can see in the UK. There is an extensive database of every film released in the UK and information on recent decisions and why they were awarded which certificate.

**THE BRITISH FILM INSTITUTE**
**www.bfi.org**
Very useful for a range of information including films on video and DVD, film education resources and publications, downloadable classroom worksheets and articles.

**BRIT MOVIE**
**www.britmovie.co.uk**
Dedicated to all aspects of British cinema with essays and articles on actors and films.

**THE FILM DISTRIBUTORS ASSOCIATION**
**www.lanchingfilms.com/cgi-bin/releases.pl**
An excellent introduction to the world of film distribution in the UK, with box office information, a list of every distributor in the UK and their recent releases, and a release schedule for every new title coming up each month.

Tread carefully however, as it is blatantly biased towards the more commercial distribution companies with the emphasis on celebrating huge box office returns and successful marketing campaigns for USA or USA/UK blockbusters (check out the review of the year 2003 section).

Current members are the five majors (BVI, Warners, UIP, Columbia Tri-Star and Fox) as well as Entertainment, UGC Films UK, Feature Film Company, Gala Films, Icon, Metrodome, Momentum and Pathé.


## FILM EDUCATION
**www.filmeducation.org**
An organisation funded by the major distributors which provides schools and colleges with advice and resources (often free) around new releases, many of them British – recent UK titles with teaching material available have included *Sylvia* and *Touching the Void*.


## THE INTERNET MOVIE DATABASE
**www.imdb.com**
Excellent resource to find information about just about any film ever made, including cast and crew credits, national and international reviews, images and posters, discussion sites, official sites of films, articles and essays and general gossip and trivia. Extremely addictive.


## SCREEN ONLINE
**www.screenonline.org.uk**
Produced by the BFI, this is a major resource for anyone interested in teaching British cinema with stills, articles, worksheets, poster art, video and audio clips from British films.


## THE UK FILM COUNCIL
**www.ukfilmcouncil.org.uk**
Full of information about how British films can be funded and regular updates on how they are doing at the UK box office.